Praise for
I Can Do That!

"Alice Potter in *I Can Do That!* is the entertaining and insightful cruise director for the cruise we all take—our life."

—George C. Wilson,
bestselling author of *Super-Carrier*,
former correspondent for *The Washington Post*

"Read the book and then re-read it and notice how you grow stronger with each page and each exercise. Then share the book with friends and loved ones and see how they too will grow! You will see how you, and your friends, will begin to do amazing things because you realized . . . *I Can Do That!*"

—Willie Jolley, author of *It Only Takes
a Minute to Change Your Life*, host of
"The Magnificent Motivational Minute"

Berkley Titles by Alice Potter

THE POSITIVE THINKER
I CAN DO THAT!

I
CAN
DO
THAT!

Alice Potter

BERKLEY BOOKS, NEW YORK

I CAN DO THAT!

A Berkley Book / published by arrangement with
the author

PRINTING HISTORY
Berkley edition / September 1997

The Putnam Berkley World Wide Web site address is
http://www.berkley.com

ISBN: 0-425-15771-7

To my grandson, Campbell—
You can do it all!

And to you—
Who can as well

Acknowledgments

First and foremost, I wish to thank my editor, Hillary Cige, and everyone at The Berkley Publishing Group for giving me the opportunity to write this book.

I could not have written this book without the many personal stories contributed by friends, relatives, colleagues and, especially, my buddies at the National Speakers Association. Since some have requested anonymity, I cannot divulge all their names here, but generous contributors include Dick Fitzmaurice, Martin Krieg, Danny Robinson, Fern Barker, Kata, Art Carlson, Jay Mulkey, Mona Martineau, Brian Lee, Annabel Marsh, Julie Church, Cathy Le Blanc, Bill Mann, Bob Modersohn, Beverly Potter, Phil Potter, Mark Potter, Michael Lee, Marianna Nunes, Joel Rutledge, Bev Bender, Shirley Nice, Shirley Carolan, and Allen Klein. I thank you all profusely.

Very special thanks go to the members of my writer's support group, Allen Klein, Lynn Fraley, and Bob Coleman, whose ongoing suggestions and unfailing inspiration encouraged me to continue searching until I came up with the appropriate vehicle in which to express this philosophy.

I also wish to thank Dorothy Wall for her helpful, insightful critique on parts of my first draft, and Jay Mulkey for his efforts on my behalf. Last but far from least, I extend endless thanks to my good friend, the very talented Elena Facciola, who illustrated this book.

Contents

PART ONE

Exploring and Analyzing

PART TWO

Getting Down to Business

PART THREE
Doing It

I
CAN
DO
THAT!

Introduction

Far away in the sunshine are my highest aspirations.
I may not reach them, but I can look up and see their
beauty,
believe in them, and try to follow where they lead.

—*Louisa May Alcott*

We are about to start on a grand adventure, one that we will take together. Our destination is Utopia, Shangri La, Paradise—or whatever defines heaven on earth to you. It will not be an easy voyage. Our trip will cover some rocky territory; there will be valleys and mountains—flat, barren spots and brilliant areas of enlightenment.

You will be a different person when you complete this journey; you'll be more decisive, optimistic, and confident. You'll discover exactly what you want in life and you'll learn how to achieve those goals. And you'll identify where you're going and how to get there.

After this experience, your life will be forever changed for the better. There'll be many lessons learned along the way; some may be easy, others more difficult. It will be fun and frustrating, satisfying and rewarding, exciting, enlightening, and informative.

I will be your guide, but you will do most of the work. At the end of our journey, you will be a new person, the one you've always wanted to be and have dreamed of becoming. You will learn how to set goals and accomplish them. You'll be encouraged to dream, and you'll discover that dreams can come true.

You'll learn from the experiences of many who've shared their personal stories with me, and I'll tell you of some of my own successes and failures. The stories herein are true; most were contributed by friends, relatives, and colleagues, all ordinary people like you and me; others were gleaned from inspiring newspaper articles. In some cases, friends asked that I not reveal their true identities, but for the most part, actual names are given.

You will be inspired by the accomplishments documented here; some are relatively minor, others are on a major scale. The point is that all accomplishments, regardless of magnitude, are victories and must be celebrated and honored as such. As you read of the struggles and ultimate successes of others, you'll be encouraged to approach and conquer yours—to reach for your goals, dreams, and desires—for they can and will manifest for you.

Ponder This

If one advances confidently in the direction of his dreams, and endeavors to live the life which he has imagined, he will meet with a success unexpected in common hours.

—*Henry David Thoreau*

The Beginning

I Was Anonymous

Manifest plainness,
Embrace simplicity,
Reduce selfishness,
Have few desires.

—*Lao-tzu*

When I was a child and a young girl, I was brought up by the maxim, "Young ladies are to be seen and not heard." Certainly I was not heard because I hardly ever said a word; I was probably the quietest child in my class, perhaps the entire school. But I also felt that I was not seen; sometimes I felt downright invisible.

Why did I feel this way? Even today, that's hard for me to explain; perhaps I still don't totally understand. But I do have some thoughts on those impressionable years, years that were, to me, frustrating and vaguely empty.

I think the word "anonymous" describes my early life perfectly. Webster defines anonymous as "lacking marked individuality or personality." That also defines the young Alice. I certainly lacked marked individuality and personality.

But how could a young person, trained to sit quietly and speak mainly when spoken to, display marked individuality

or much of a personality? I was not encouraged to speak out or have opinions; those things were reserved for the males of this world. Women were to be compliant, agreeable, inconspicuous, subservient, and bow to the opinions of the dominant male of the household. As a child, that male was my father. I understood that when I married, the dominant role would fall to my husband. My role would continue to be the same: to be compliant, agreeable, inconspicuous, subservient, and unobtrusive. To be otherwise was not to be considered.

Somehow, I absorbed the fact that people in general, and men in particular, did not like women who displayed any sort of assertiveness. Having opinions, accomplishing unusual things, succeeding in any area other than wifeliness and motherhood were not only not encouraged, they were actively discouraged.

I don't ever remember saying, "I can do that!" and having anyone reply, "Great idea. Of course you can!" Instead, I heard all the negatives about my spoken desire. "What makes *you* think you can do that?" "You're too young, too small, you're just a girl." "That sort of thing is only for athletes, other people, the wealthy, the famous." I think my parents discouraged me from trying new and challenging things because they wanted to protect me from failure.

But mainly, my mother, in her infinite caring and concern, wanted to protect me from harm. Almost anything new, different, challenging, or adventurous represented harm to my mother. To her, it was important for me to be anonymous; in that way, I wouldn't be noticed or stand out. I wouldn't be singled out for admiration, adulation, applause, or awards. To wear makeup made one stand out. To wear a brightly colored outfit made one stand out. To come in first, win a competition or contest, or to be chosen for something special made one stand out. To succeed made one stand out.

What harm could possibly come from being noticed or standing out? One might be followed, attacked, raped, or kidnapped, of course! One might attract undesirable types: gigolos, insincere people, and those with "no good" on their minds. Any number of dire and dreadful things might ensue. Better to be invisible, to fade into the background. Better to be anonymous. Better to be safe.

In this day and age, that fear might have merit, but when I was growing up in the protective environment of small-town America, crime and all the other bad stuff so prevalent today was virtually unknown. Perhaps mother had an insight into the future.

In addition, exhibiting bravado by saying, "I can do that," and succeeding, was bound to bring on bragging and conceit, traits not appropriate for young ladies who were meant to be seen and not heard. Self-esteem, a term I never heard in my childhood, would probably have been equated with vanity and ego in my parents' opinion. Vanity, in any form, was the attribute my mother feared most in her daughters. Egos were to be squashed for fear of offending. One could not be vain or egotistical and still be compliant, agreeable, inconspicuous, and subservient. One could not be conceited and maintain friends. Better to be inoffensive. Better to be anonymous, invisible, safe.

Better *never* to say "I can do that" and succeed.

And that's the way I lived my life for the first twenty-eight years.

Ponder This

The mass of men lead lives of quiet desperation.
What is called resignation is confirmed desperation.

—Henry David Thoreau

PART ONE

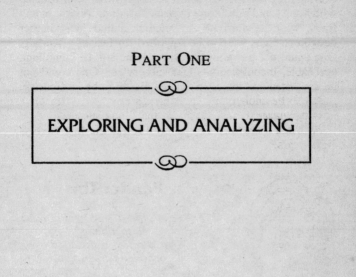

EXPLORING AND ANALYZING

1

I Can Do That

A Personal Story

What would you attempt to do if you knew you could not fail?

—Dr. Robert Schuller

There I was, twenty-eight years old and scared to death. I was no longer in the secure role of wife and mother in which I thought I'd be forever. Now I was a young widow, a single parent with two young children, and the designated breadwinner for our small family. I don't know which of the three new roles terrified me most: being a widow with no one but myself to rely on, the responsibility of being a single parent, or the overwhelming prospect of having to work to support myself and my children. The latter appeared to be the most pressing.

But me? Become a working woman? You've got to be kidding! Mothers didn't work in the mid-fifties. I was raised to be a wife and mother, nothing else, and my macho military husband had perpetuated the "wives don't work" attitude of my parents. I'd never been employed nor ever expected to be, my education was limited, and I had no job skills whatsoever. But the bottom line said, "Alice must get a job!"

"There's got to be something I can do," I reasoned. Then I remembered my volunteer work as a Gray Lady at military hospitals where we'd been stationed. "Maybe I can become a doctor's assistant or receptionist." I certainly didn't know how to do anything else, or so I thought. So I went to the newspaper classifieds and lo and behold, there was a Help Wanted ad for a doctor's assistant–receptionist! *I can do that*, I thought to myself. I must have exuded enough confidence in the interview because, to my surprise, I was hired instantly and started to work the very next day.

The job was easy, no special skills were required, and everything went well for a month or so, but I could see a big problem developing. My doctor was new in the community and had just hung up his shingle; consequently, he had few patients. I was a young, attractive, very naive widow. There was too much alone time with just the two of us in the office. Daily, I became more and more nervous about his personal remarks and increasing attempts at closeness. Wisely, before things got too sticky, I gave him notice and went back to the classifieds.

Next, I found myself employed as a receptionist–girl Friday in a brokerage firm. Again, I found myself in a two-person office, but this one had a huge wall-sized window facing the street. I confidently hoped that would thwart any future attempts at unsolicited hanky-panky. "Stick with me, kid," Bert, my broker promised. "You're just a gal Friday now, but down the road, I can make you the first woman stockbroker in northern New York!" I hated figures and finance with a passion, but the term "lady stockbroker" had a prestigious ring to it. Maybe, instead of just being an office worker, I'd found myself a career field. Career! That word had never entered my vocabulary before.

One night, I went out to dinner with a new friend, and afterward we sat in the car listening to the radio and talking. The pleasant mood was broken by the gravelly voice of the announcer, his inane remarks, and the poor choice of music.

"Listen to that!" I exploded. "Can you believe that radio station! Why in heavens name would they allow someone like that on the air at this time of night?"

"What do you suggest?" asked my friend in an amused tone, whereupon I went on to suggest a lot of things, including the fact that a soothing voice, preferably a woman's, would be much more appropriate. Before the conversation was over, I found myself adamantly declaring, "I can do that!" In fact, I said I'd undoubtedly do a far better job than the sorry DJ we were listening to. We'd had some wine with dinner; no doubt that's why my normal reticence and modesty were a bit lax. Whatever the reason for my unusually outspoken comments, I'm forever grateful. Unknowingly, that was one of the most important conversations of my entire life.

The next morning I was at my desk at the brokerage when the phone rang. It was my friend of the night before. "Do you remember our conversation of last night? The part about the radio station?"

"Oh, vaguely," I answered. "Why?

"Well, I didn't tell you then, but I know the owner and the manager of the station we were listening to. I just told them about you and your ideas about nighttime radio. They're interested in meeting you. Can you come up to the station during your lunch hour?"

Could I? Get to see the inside of a real radio station? See show biz in action? Wild horses couldn't stop me!

Then it hit me. Someone wanted to hear *my* ideas! I was astounded. What could I—anonymous, invisible Alice— contribute? Who was I to be so brash as to even consider telling broadcast professionals how to run their business?

Desperately trying to remember my outburst of the night before and my resultant ideas, I raced to the station. I had never been in a radio station before in my life, and when I opened the door and walked in, I was absolutely mesmerized by what I saw. There, across from the entryway, was a glass room. Inside this glass room—I found out it's called a studio—sat a man with earphones on. There was a turntable on either side of him, a microphone in front of his face, and he was surrounded by stacks of record albums

and tapes. *That has got to be the most exciting, glamorous job in the whole wide world!* I thought.

I joined my friend, the station owner, Joel Shirer, and the manager, Don Pelkey, in the front office. "We understand you have ideas about improving our late-night programming," one of them said. "We'd like to hear them."

I struggled to reconstruct the conversation of the previous evening. Fortunately, my mouth went into gear and I surprised myself by saying, "You need Alice in Slumberland on your air!" Where I came up with that title I'll never know, but thank goodness for on-the-spot inspiration!

"Do you have a tape recorder?" Don asked.

I had one left over from my husband's Korean tour of duty; we'd communicated by tape as well as mail.

"How about putting a sample program on tape," Don

suggested. "The whole thing: intro, theme, music . . ."

A sample program? He wants *me* to put a sample program on tape? That someone would ask me to actually put my money where my mouth was, so to speak, floored me. "Oh, sure, I can do that," I heard myself exclaim. My voice with its positive, upbeat note seemed far removed from me.

"Oh, and don't forget the commercials," Don added.

"Commercials?" I asked, bewildered.

"Yeah, you know, those sixty-second advertisements."

"Uh, sure . . . I can do that . . ." I mumbled, wondering if I actually could. I felt as if I were in a dream state and I didn't want to wake up.

That evening, I headed for the record store. I picked "Street of Dreams" by Les and Larry Elgart for my theme song, and some albums I thought appropriate for the body of the sample program. I was stumped momentarily in the commercial-writing department, then I thought of the Yellow Pages; there I'd find all the information needed for writing those "sixty-second advertisements." The challenge scared me in one way but excited me in another. *Nothing ventured, nothing gained,* I thought, as my excitement over the project mounted.

You can't believe the amateurish tape I put together! I simply held the recorder mike up to the record player for the music and, in between playing bits of music and reading my commercials, I purred what I thought were appropriate comments for the midnight hour. It was hard to stifle the giggles as I pretended to be sexy and seductive in my delivery. When I felt I had my best effort on tape, I called Don Pelkey.

This time, when I arrived at the station, instead of going into the manager's office, I was ushered into a large conference room. To my horror, the entire staff was assembled: the owner, the manager, the program director, the entire sales staff, all the announcers except for the man on duty, even the receptionist. This appeared to be a family-type operation.

Oh my God! I thought as I looked for a place to hide. *What have I gotten myself into?* As my tape played, instead of the laughter I expected, I noticed the listeners were serious, nodding to each other.

Then Don asked, "Can you sell?"

"Sell what?" I asked, perplexed.

"Airtime," Don explained. "Just go up and down Main Street and talk to all the business owners or managers and tell them about your program. Explain how, if they advertise with you, they'll bring in lots of new customers and increase their business . . . stuff like that."

"That's selling?" I asked, astonished. It sounded so easy. "Oh, I can do that!"

"Here's a rate card, a pad of contracts, and there's the street," instructed Don. "Come back when you've sold three thirteen-week contracts."

Three thirteen-week contracts? I can do better than that, I thought with innocent optimism. Enthusiasm is wonderful; I sold ten contracts. Good-bye brokerage! With tremendous relief, I realized how much I actually hated that type of business. And to think I'd almost considered it seriously as a career field.

I didn't realize it at the time, but Don wasn't as excited about Alice in Slumberland and my titillating his nighttime audience as he was about the new revenues coming in for a time period that had never sold before. That really didn't matter in the long run; we both got what we wanted out of my late-night program: a true win-win situation.

In retrospect and considering my background, I wonder at my boldness. Bert, my broker, warned me about the hazards of "the glitzy world of show business." Sounding fatherly, he cautioned me about the many pitfalls ahead, the slick, untrustworthy characters I'd come into contact with, the heartaches, the traumas, the audition couches, and disillusionment that were sure to come. With wide-eyed optimism, and oblivious to his dire predictions, I thanked him for his concern and charged ahead, never once looking back. In my inner being, I knew this was right for me.

You, too, will experience that clear-cut knowledge when you find your life's true path. The chapters ahead promise to show you the way.

Alice in Slumberland went on the air two weeks later. Nightly, I spun records in the glass room. I could hardly believe it. Me! In the glass room! I was a DJ just like the announcer I saw the first time I ever visited a radio station.

Then the mail started coming in.

> "Dear Alice, We listen to you every night. Will you send us some pictures for our walls?
>
> Signed: The Boys from Cell Block 2, Dannemora State Prison."

> "Dear Alice, I listen to you every night. When you do that mattress commercial, I feel right frisky.
>
> Signed: Grandpa."

> "Dear Alice, I listen to you every night. How do you feel about younger men?
>
> Signed: Johnny, Plattsburgh High School."

No one knew who Alice was. The radio station never divulged my name. Local folks spoke of Alice as "the sex kitten of the airwaves." In this instance, it was great fun being anonymous; even more fun being considered a sex kitten.

My daughter, by now a budding teenager, had just entered Plattsburgh Junior High School. She was embarrassed to tears over the situation. "Mother," she wailed, "all those pimply faced creeps at school are fantasizing about Alice in Slumberland. I'm mortified!"

"But no one knows who Alice is," I reminded her.

"Well, I do," she retorted, stamping her foot and flouncing out of the room as only a teenager can do.

A short time later, I heard about auditions for a happy homemaker–type show at the local TV station. Now, that was right up my alley. I can do that! If anyone knew about homemaking, it was yours truly. Flushed with pride at my recent accomplishments, I exuded confidence at the audition. Next thing I knew, I was Alice in Slumberland, radio sex kitten, at night, and Alice Potter, Happy Homemaker, daily from 1:15 to 2 on TV. Amazingly, no one ever made the connection.

Soon, my naive I-can-do-that attitude propelled me into other broadcast ventures. I began doing voice-overs, on-camera commercials, and other types of programs. Eventually, I felt I'd saturated the local market and started looking for new opportunities. Various assignments took me through Middle America. I was a weather girl, a Vanna White game show type, a talk show host at several TV stations, an expert in airtime sales and, eventually, I became the general manager of two radio stations and a TV station. I understand I was the first woman general manager of a commercial radio station in the entire country. Each step of the way, each advancement was preceded by an enthusiastic "I can do that!"

"I can do that!" truly turned out to be a magic phrase for me as you can tell by reading my story. It totally changed my life from one of a predicted, mundane existence to one of fun, excitement, challenge, and fulfillment. "I can do that!" can be your key to the life you've always dreamed about as well. You'll learn how to put it to work for you as you progress through this book. For now, just practice saying the magic phrase, "I can do that!" whenever you're faced with a challenge, whether it's large or small.

All in all, I spent twenty years in radio and television broadcasting. And never for a minute did I ever regret my career field. But how did it happen? Was it an accident that my friend and I listened to a gravelly voiced disc jockey one Sunday evening after dinner? Was it an accident that I became so passionate about what that station should be air-

ing? Was it an accident that my friend knew the people at the radio station, that they took me seriously, and gave me the opportunity of my lifetime? Could my innocent optimism, my enthusiastic I-can-do-that attitude have had anything to do with it? Or was there someone looking over my shoulder who said, "Let's give Alice a chance." A chance at life, happiness, success, and one of the greatest careers in the world: broadcasting. I like to think it was a combination of the above. Definitely, saying "I can do that" and believing it, combined with some luck and divine intervention, perhaps, resulted in the philosophy I will share with you in the following pages.

My Alice in Slumberland theme song, "Street of Dreams," was so very appropriate. Nightly I opened my program over the strains of the song by saying, "Hello, this is Alice, Alice in Slumberland. Won't you come with me down the street of dreams?"

It's important to find *your* street of dreams and follow it. You'll never be sorry. It's equally important to be optimistic, enthusiastic, and truly believe in yourself when you say, ''I can do that!''

At the moment, you may be having doubts about your ability to accomplish your goals and manifest your dreams, but let me assure you that if I, Anonymous Alice, could do it, *you can, too!* Yes, even though I was brought up to stay in the shadows, to be invisible, there was a spark in me that I didn't know existed until something happened to fan the flame. We all, each and every one of us, have that vital spark. Even if it's only a tiny, faint flame at the moment, it can be kindled and brought to life. My purpose, through this book, is to fan the flame of your life spark and make it shine brightly.

I told you my story, but we all come from different backgrounds and beginnings. You, too, as I, may have had people, circumstances, and experiences in your life that contributed to your personal self-doubt or lack of confidence. All of that will change as we journey together through the pages of this book to an exciting new place of self-discovery, success, and total fulfillment.

Your "I Can Do" Review

Reread the preceding story of my entry into broadcasting to observe how many times I said, ''I can do that,'' often without realizing the importance of the phrase.

Notice that each time I said it, each challenge, even though small, helped to build my confidence in myself. Know that you can apply this basic principle to your life *right now.*

Realize that in small matters as well as large, ''I can do that!'' is sheer magic. Properly used, ''I can do that'' can make your dreams and desires become actualities.

Begin to think about your dreams, the things you'd like

to accomplish if, as Dr. Robert Schuller says, "you knew you could not fail." Start a list of those dreams and aspirations here.

_____

_____

_____

_____

_____

Ponder This

You can have anything you want if you want it desperately enough. You must want it with an inner exuberance that erupts through the skin and joins the energy that created the world.

—Shiela Graham

2

No I Can't

Exploring Doubts, Excuses, and Delays

The future belongs to those who believe in the beauty of their dreams.

—*Eleanor Roosevelt*

"Well, I can't do the things I want to do," I hear you saying. "My dreams are too big, my problems too great. I'm lucky just to stay afloat in my personal daily grind without going off on some tangent like entering a glamorous profession such as broadcasting. Get with the real world, Alice!"

Whoa! Hold it! Sharing my story with you was just an illustration of the power of four little words, "I can do that!" Innocuous as it may seem, the phrase "I can do that" is powerful. Once stated, it can be a challenge, a motivator, a relentless nagging voice that demands that you, in fact, "do that."

"I can do that" is an affirmation that you can always turn to when you want to get the job done. This is positive thinking in its purest, most convincing form. Once uttered, "I can do that" will not go away. It is obstinate, emphatic, and dictatorial.

"I can do that" can apply to the most minute of life's objectives as well as to the grandest, most challenging goal in your life. Applied in minute doses, starting with small ambitions that are likely to be fulfilled, it can build your confidence to the point where large aspirations and challenges are approached with confidence, and thereby lead—ultimately—to success.

That said, let's explore some of the doubts and fears you have about doing what you really want to do, and some of your self-imposed delays. We'll also look into your litany of excuses because, if you're like the rest of us, you have dozens of reasons why you're not "doing that."

What are some of the things most people say they want to do, but don't—or, according to them, *can't*—do? "I want to lose weight" probably heads the list and that universal desire is followed closely by "I want to stop smoking." According to a year-end poll by *U.S. News & World Report*, losing weight is the top New Year's resolution for women. Men's top resolution is to quit smoking and, for them, losing weight is only one percentage point behind.

If you fall into either of those groups, what are you doing about it? What are you *really* doing about losing weight or stopping smoking? Regarding the weight issue, Jane told me, "I'm trying to lose a few pounds, but it's hard. I'm expected to cook beautiful, nourishing meals for my husband and kids, and I like doing that. But they want mashed potatoes and gravy, pies, cookies, and cinnamon buns; all the things I shouldn't eat; naturally I want to please them. How am I supposed to lose weight under those circumstances? I'm trying to diet, but it's the yo-yo thing. I lose a few pounds, then I put them all back on, plus more. Every year, losing weight is my primary New Year's resolution. Then, when I fail, I get so discouraged with myself, I just plain give up. Sometimes I even go on an eating binge; naturally, that only makes things worse. But, I'm trying. I really am!"

I talked to Alan about his smoking habit. "I've tried to quit a thousand times. Sometimes I can get through a whole week without a cigarette, but then I'm hell to live with: nervous, cranky, and downright disagreeable. My family wants me to quit because that secondhand smoke we hear so much about really gets to them. And they're worried about my health. While I don't tell them, I'm worried, too. I know my health is suffering. I actually feel rotten most of the time. And this cough, it just won't go away. But I'm trying to cut down to just a few smokes a day. I tried the patches; they didn't work. Maybe I'll try hypnosis next. It's worth a try.''

Money problems and getting out of debt are right up there on many people's want-to-do list next to losing weight and quitting smoking. Carolyn is a compulsive shopper. She cannot control her spending. Hiding her new purchases and bills from her husband has become a monumental problem. ''I want to get out of debt in the worst way,'' she confided to me, ''but I just can't seem to control myself. Shopping is my downfall. I shop when I'm bored. I shop when I'm unhappy. And I shop when I'm happy, too. I really don't need most of the stuff I buy, but I sure feel good when I'm buying it! Then come the lies. Jim asks me where this or that came from. I tell him someone gave me something they didn't want or, if it's an article of clothing, that it's been in the closet for ages and he must have forgotten about it. We did the debt consolidation thing once; they made me cut up my charge cards. Do you know how easy it is to get more? Jim doesn't know about my new accounts. But it's going to catch up with me, and soon. I didn't pay our estimated taxes and we're behind in our mortgage payments. If Jim finds out about that, plus the extent of my new charge card debts, he'll divorce me for sure. I've really tried to cut back, but I can't seem to do it. There must be something new I can try.''

Carolyn is an exception. Most people's money problems are not quite as self-inflicted as hers are, although runaway spending is always a contributing factor. If money and the lack of a sufficient amount, or the proper handling of it, is a problem in your life, what are you doing about it? ''I'm trying to stick to my budget,'' is the usual response. Then comes the inevitable ''but.'' ''But one of the kids needs braces.'' ''But my wife was laid off.'' ''But the furnace went out." "But the car broke down." But ad infinitum.

"But" is one of the two insidious three-letter words that can get in the way of your doing what you want to do. Life is full of buts. There's no way we can control our "but" contingencies. We must learn how to contend with them, however, when they rear their ugly heads and get in the way of our goals. We must realize that our buts are convenient excuses, our hoped-for way of explaining our way out of a problem, of avoiding responsibility. Sometimes we need that cushion; life is hard and we need a way of getting off the hook. The important thing with buts, especially if you seem to have an undue number in your life, is to analyze them and see if you can reverse the phrase they occupy and turn it into a positive.

For example, instead of "I want to ask for a raise, but I'm afraid to rock the boat; I might get fired for asking," think about saying, "I'm going to ask for a raise, and I plan to show the boss an account of my previous accomplishments and the ways I can increase company production in the future." In this example we changed "want," which is wishful thinking, to "going to," which shows intention. Then we changed "but," our excuse word, to "and" followed by the action step, which will go far to insure the raise.

The other insidious three-letter word is "try." Jane, Alan, and Carolyn are very familiar with "try." Jane is "trying" to lose weight and has been "trying" for most of her adult life. Alan has been "trying" to quit smoking for years. Carolyn says she's "trying" to control her spending in order to save her marriage. If you, as well as Jane, Alan, and Carolyn stop "trying" and start "doing," goals will soon begin to become realities. We'll learn how as we progress through the chapters to come.

For now, let's put a Band-Aid on one of the above problems, that of excess smoking. You know you've been consuming too many cigarettes, but you're not ready to go "cold turkey" right now, you just want to cut back. Perhaps you've been saying, "I've been trying to cut back on

my smoking, but with the stresses on my job, I always end up smoking two packs a day.'' Here we've got both ''trying'' and ''but'' in your sentence about your desire to cut back. Better to say, ''I'm cutting back on my cigarette consumption. When I feel stressed, I go to the water cooler for a drink or suck on a lozenge.''

Note that you've replaced the ineffective ''trying'' with a definite statement: ''I'm cutting back on my cigarette consumption.'' Then, rather than your old ''but'' excuse, you institute a substitute action step, that of getting a drink of water or using a lozenge instead of lighting up a cigarette. It might also be helpful to look carefully at the stress triggers that bring on your desire to smoke. Is there any way you can cut back or eliminate them?

"But" is offering an excuse, albeit often valid, for not doing. To "try" is "to make an attempt at." It is also not doing. Yoda said, "Do or do not. There is no try." If you are going to do the things you want to in your life, if you want to achieve the goals you've set for yourself, if you hope to get out of your self-imposed rut, you've got to minimize your "buts" and eliminate your "try's" by changing them to "I can do's."

Please don't misunderstand. I'm not minimizing the difficulty of losing weight, quitting smoking, or controlling spending. These are exceedingly difficult challenges faced by millions of people, and it helps to know that you are not alone in fighting the battle. Be easy on yourself. Remind yourself that nobody's perfect. For now, accept yourself exactly as you are. At the moment, we're just exploring the doubts, excuses, and delays that seem to continually get in the way of you doing what you want to do. Later, we'll address these issues and see what we can do about eliminating them.

Flat-out "I can'ts" are quite prevalent in the excuse department. Almost anything on your "I want to do that" list can be followed with "But I can't." They say the thing most people fear, perhaps more than death, is speaking in front of a group. Often, speaking in front of a group, however small, can be a requirement of your job. You have to make a presentation in front of the board or the sales staff. What happens? You get weak in the knees, your palms get sweaty, and you say, "I can't!" And you don't. Or your presentation is so ineffective that you've actually lost ground in the eyes of your superiors. Are "I can'ts" causing problems in your life or career? If so, you can do something about it. Keep reading, and I'll show you how.

John took early retirement from a government job in order to do the things he really wanted to do in his life. He took courses in financial planning and tax preparation, and now he has a small, but growing clientele. He works out of his home at hours he personally sets. It's an ideal situation for John. Things are going well but, as John confessed to me, "I can't remember names. It's so embarrassing! I ran into a client on the street the other day, and I couldn't introduce him to the friend I was with." I asked John if he really made an effort to remember his clients' names. "I just can't remember names. That's just the way it is! I've never been able to remember names. It's simply something I can't do. I remember faces, though. I never forget a face!" John needs to realize that the sound of one's own name is the sweetest sound in the world. His accounting business would definitely improve if he could get over his self-imposed "I can't" and made a sincere effort to remember his clients' names.

One way John could get over his negativity about remembering his clients' names is to make a *personal commitment* to himself to remember their names. Personal commitments can be very powerful; breaking a commitment you've made to yourself can bring on feelings of guilt and remorse. Why do that to yourself? If John would say "I can and I will remember my clients' names," he'd be off on the right foot. His saying "I can" forcefully and with meaning would be a strong antidote to his former, negative "I can't." Then, John could follow through by repeating his clients' names throughout his conversations with them and by writing their names down and consciously associating their names with their faces, which are easy for him to remember. He could also take a memory course or read books on improving one's memory.

In addition to "buts," "trys," and "I can'ts," other excuses and delays in achieving your life's goals and desires are often due to "If only's." You get to fill in the blanks in the following examples:

If only I were younger/older/taller/shorter/thinner/smarter, I'd _____.

If only I were a man/a woman/white/black, I'd _____.

If only I'd finished college/studied harder/read more books, I'd _____.

If only I'd listened to my parents/not listened to my parents/paid more attention to my teachers, I'd _____.

If only I'd been born into a wealthy family/had the advantages of the affluent, I'd _____.

What are some of your "if only's?" Perhaps, if they're similar to some of the above, you might counter them this way: In regard to being younger/older, taller/shorter, etc., as well as worrying about the gender/color issue, you might say to yourself repeatedly, "I'm perfect the way I am!" Regarding the educational issues presented by the college/studying/reading "if only" example, realize that you can still broaden your education through a variety of means, including reading, which will not bankrupt your bank account. As to the last complaint referring to wealth and affluence, note that many if not most of the world's movers and shakers did not come from wealthy families. They did it on their own. So can you. Read biographies of some of the individuals you admire and follow their examples.

"If only's," like "buts" and "trys," are excuses, pure and simple. "If only's" usually refer to the past about which we can do nothing, they often refer to things over which we have little or no control, and they frequently blame others for our own failures or shortcomings. Don't let the past control your future. Get rid of the "if only's" in your life and your vocabulary. "If only's" have no place in the mind of an "I can do that" person. For now, be aware of how many times you find yourself saying "if only." Know that by the time you finish this book, that excuse phrase will be absent from your vocabulary.

While you're cleaning out your mental house, plan to eliminate "I'll do that (the thing you *really* want to do) later, when . . ." "Do that" in this case is often synonymous with "I'll get around to that and then I'll be happy." Examples:

I'll be happy when I graduate from high school/college/ get my degree.

I'll be happy when I get a job.

I'll be happy when I get married.

I'll be happy when we have children.

I'll be happy when the kids are in school.

I'll be happy when the kids are off on their own.

I'll be happy when I retire.

I'll be happy when (name of spouse) is home from the hospital and well again.

I'll be happy when my grandkids visit me in the nursing home.

And so it goes.

Please note the future tense in all the above statements is exaggerated a bit to make a point. Delayed gratification has its merits, but for a lifetime? What about now? Get on the "now" bandwagon—and get on it *now!* Do it—whatever it is that you want to do—now. The late Michael Landon, one of this country's favorite and most beloved TV stars, said prophetically, "Do it now! There are only so many tomorrows."

One way to start now is to think about something you really want to accomplish. Start with something small, something relatively easy that isn't too intimidating. Later, you can graduate to larger, more important goals. If you're stuck, I can furnish a few easy "I want to" examples to get you started:

Balance my checkbook

Learn to program my VCR

Start a mini exercise program—15 minutes per day

Read books that will help me in my career and personal life

Organize my desk

Call my parents/children once a week

Remember to smile at grocery checkers, bank tellers, postal clerks, and other harried people

Pay my bills on time

These are all relatively easy-to-accomplish tasks, except for the one about the VCR. That's been on my to-do-list for some time now. I have not put myself to the test and said, "I can do that!" because the thing intimidates me, and I'm not yet ready. I threw it in this list because it sounded like it might appeal to some of you brave, adventurous types.

Think about what it is you want to accomplish, or the example you've chosen for this exercise. Then say, "I can do that!" Say it out loud. How does it feel? How do you feel? Hopefully, you feel good about making a commitment about something positive, regardless of how minor it might be. If you feel uncomfortable, please don't get uptight about it; this is only a test.

Your "I Can Do" Review

Think about the dreams and aspirations you listed at the end of chapter 1. Then, to the best of your recollection, note if any of the following kept you from following through on your desires.

I "tried" or I am still "trying" to:

_____

_____

_____

I was working toward those goals, "but":

_____

_____

_____

I find myself saying "if only" about:

_____

_____

_____

I continually seem to say "I can't" about the following:

_____

_____

_____

I constantly delay doing what I want to do because:

_____

_____

_____

If stresses at home or on the job seem to be a factor, note here if you think that you can take steps to eliminate or diminish those stresses.

_____

_____

_____

Ponder This

If you think you can, or if you think you can't, you're right.

—Henry Ford

3

Do I Have to Do Everything?

Honoring Individual Talents and Desires

> *This above all:*
> *to thine own self be true,*
> *And it must follow,*
> *as the night the day.*
> *Thou canst not then be false*
> *to any man.*
>
> *—Shakespeare*

I had a conversation with Mark when this book was in its conceptual stages. Mark is an attorney; although very creative, he is mainly intelligent, logical, rational and, as most attorneys, a left-brain thinker. He plays the role of devil's advocate very well.

Mark questioned me, "If, as you suggest, saying and truly believing 'I can do that' will allow people to achieve all of their goals, wouldn't everyone end up doing everything? Wouldn't everyone aspire to climb the highest mountains, sail all the challenging seas, fly around the world at record-breaking speeds, win Olympic gold medals, find cures for diseases that are presently incurable, and on and on? In other words, wouldn't everyone face and overcome every challenge the world has to offer because they believe they can do it? Then there'd be no victory, no thrill, no glory in succeeding, no feeling of individual accomplishment."

We had a lively discussion about individual accomplishment and the foolishness of aspiring to do it all. I explained to my devil's advocate that he misunderstood my premise in writing this book and encouraging people to say, "I can do that!" In the first place, people are terribly occupied with the everyday requirements of life. Even if so inclined, who would have the time, energy, or resources to succeed at *every one* of life's challenges? But, even if time, energy, and resources were no problem, who would *want* to do all of those things? "I can do that!" only applies to each individual's *personal challenges, desires, and talents.* "I can do that" only works with each individual's *personal passion.*

My friend Hans is a marathon runner. Contrary to the confusion in some people's minds, a marathon is 26.2 miles. It is always 26.2 miles whether the marathon is run in Boston, New York, Los Angeles, Paris, London, Berlin, or anywhere else. Running 26.2 miles is a grueling endeavor; the human body was not made to punish itself with such a feat, yet thousands upon thousands of runners compete regularly in marathons all over the world.

Hans has run twenty-five marathons. In order to participate, he must train for months before each race. He regularly suffers injuries to his feet, knees, and other body parts during training and during the race itself. He completed the Los Angeles Marathon in 1988 with a broken leg. He has had numerous surgeries, major and minor, caused by his running, and yet he still keeps running. Hans has a *passion* for running in general and marathons in particular. That is his thing, not mine. Running, marathons, and other competitive races is also a passion for many thousands of people worldwide.

I would not attempt to run a marathon, regardless of the payment or reward offered. I reserve the right to say "I can't" in regard to marathons, because that is true. I cannot, will not, run a marathon! I honor Hans's desire to run marathons; he honors my refusal to do so. It would be foolish for me to risk bodily injury by participating in a sport or activity such as marathoning if I didn't have a passion for

it. Why should I when there are so many other things I do have a passion for?

What is *your* passion? That's a tough question, sometimes. Webster defines passion as "a strong liking for or devotion to some activity, object or concept." Does that help clarify things? Let's explore the passions of some of my friends and acquaintences; perhaps that will help you to identify yours. Please don't be intimidated by what others do. Rember Mark's concern: you're not expected to do everything—only your own thing.

My high-school friend, Art Carlson, is a self-taught photographer whose goal is to become a landscape photographer along the lines of Ansel Adams. Art has a talent for photography—black-and-white photography—as did Adams. More importantly, like his famous role model, Art has a *passion* for photography. Like John from chapter 2 who says he can't remember names, Art also took early retirement to go into business for himself. In Art's case, it was the photography business. In 1990, his new vocation-avocation took him from New Jersey to Florida, Arizona, and Canada and back; in 1993, on another three-month photo tour, he went all the way from the East Coast to Alaska in his search for suitable subjects to photograph. Art does his own developing and printing and all his own matting, mounting, and framing. When asked about that tremendous output of effort, Art says, "It's all a labor of love." Looking at his work, that is obvious. Now, Art displays the photographic results of his trips at various galleries throughout the Northeast. He'll be off soon on another photo shoot; this time to England and Scotland. Art is having the time of his life, working and following his passion.

As with marathoning, photography is not for everyone. I rarely take pictures because I don't have the patience or knowledge to deal with complex equipment. The simple cameras are a breeze, but I still manage to cut off heads, feet, or other important elements of the subject. So I let others take the pictures while I enjoy the fruits of their more expert output.

I mentioned John, my "I can't remember names" friend a couple of times. Let me bring him up again now to discuss his passions: financial planning and tax preparation. These are very worthy endeavors, *if* you happen to be passionate about them. Figures, especially when related to everyone's most hated subject, taxes, leave me not only cold but downright uncomfortable. It amazes me that someone as normal as John could become passionate about taxes and finance. But many people are passionate about finance, and more power to them. Those are the ones who will come close to amassing a fortune, or at least a substantial estate, while I blunder on, trying my best to ignore the obvious. I am happy to hire John, even if he can't remember my name, to handle these matters for me. Thank goodness there are people like John, with his passion, who are available to assist people like me!

Are you getting a feel for your passion? Are you beginning to recognize it? Take a moment to think about your personal hot buttons as well as activities and concepts that stimulate and excite you. Start a mental list. Take as long as you like; you're not being timed on this. And don't be influenced by the passions of others; be true to yourself.

Another of my high school classmates, Eileen Schauler, is a professional singer of the highest caliber. Ours was a class full of vibrant people, obviously! Talent should be Eileen's middle name; she exudes it. Eileen graduated from Juilliard with the highest award in singing; she has had leading roles in operas, operettas, and musicals on this country's most prestigious stages from Broadway and Lincoln Center to Carnegie Hall and others nationwide. She performed with the New York City Opera and other illustrious companies including the Metropolitan, and was soloist with the New York Philharmonic and many major symphonies. Eileen is talent personified.

Yes, Eileen has talent, and she honors it. What are your talents? Are you honoring them? Talents may be more difficult to identify than passions, especially if you were brought up to feel talentless, as many of us were. Think about things that seem to come easy to you, things that you really enjoy doing and that you do well. They're probably true talents; you just haven't previously considered them as such. No time for modesty here. This is assessment and acknowledgement time.

It's not necessary to have a talent like Eileen's, one that will take you to the heights of a profession, in order to use and enjoy your talent. I, too, had a passion for singing at one time. The problem is, I can't sing. I don't often like to say "I can't" about anything, but the truth of the matter is, I can't sing, and I have testimonials from many to attest to that. But, because I wanted to sing so badly, so passionately, I worked at it and was in the chorus of a little theater group, sang on television, and performed at a nightclub in San Francisco and a supper club in New Jersey. Those who know me are grateful that I've moved on to other passions.

The full story of my short-lived passion for singing will come later in this book.

The point is, if you have a passion for something and/or if you have talent in some area, and you commit to doing whatever it is by saying "I can do that!" you *will* find yourself doing that. And *that* is the most exciting aspect of the entire process. Identify, commit, and do. Let those three easy-action words lead you to the realization of your dreams and goals.

I have many other talented friends whom I admire greatly for their unique capabilities. Fern and Barbara come to mind. They are both craftspeople/jewelers, but their work is totally different. Fern Barker took a class in jewelry making twenty-some years ago just to pass the time while her navy husband was away on deployment. She started out with large rings and brass neckpieces and, before long, was winning awards for her talented creations. Friends bought everything she produced, and she soon turned professional, selling her earrings and pins to fashionable boutiques. Barbara Witt, on the other hand, specializes in neckpieces to die for. Her elegant, handsome, one-of-a-kind designer conversation pieces are the rage of the rich and famous here and abroad. I understand Dinah Shore owned eight Barbara Witt masterpieces, which sell, appropriately, for prices up in the thousands. Fern and Barbara are two talented ladies who are following their passion—and it's paying off for them extremely well.

Talent comes in many forms; making people laugh is a form of talent that should be cultivated more often than it is for the pure joy it brings. I know a couple of gals, housewives and mothers, who never thought much about their talent beyond the giggles and belly laughs they provided for each other and close friends. They met almost daily in one or the other's living room and, over coffee, they cracked jokes and practiced one-liners relating to the joys, horrors, and never-ending drudgery of mommie-hood and wifedom. Encouraged by their amused neighbors and family members, they decided to try putting on skits and shows for paying audiences. Soon they were filling the rented halls with devoted followers, regaling bored and tired housewives with hilarious stories only they could truly appreciate. Before they knew it, they went nationwide, playing in theaters all over the country. Next it was guest TV appearances. Now they have their own sitcom on network TV. Perhaps you've seen Marilyn Kentz and Caryl Kristensen in *The Mommies*. Now I understand they've been signed for their own talk show. And it all started over morning coffee and a few laughs about problems and lifestyles shared by housewives and moms all over the country.

I've told you about a few of my personal friends who are talented and passionate about what they're doing with their lives. Some have turned their passions and talents into money-making ventures. Hans took early retirement to be able to do the things he really wants to do, primarily running marathons and bicycling. Art and John also took early retirement; Art to pursue photography and John to start a new career in the area of financial planning and tax preparation. Eileen doesn't perform as regularly as she used to, but she's actively involved with the American Musical and Dramatic Academy and has a large retinue of private students. Fern and Barbara continue to be as busy as they want to be following their lucrative, creative pathways. And Marilyn and Caryl hit the big time simply by making people laugh.

Except for the singing, which I managed to get out of my system some time ago, I don't have a passion for, or talent in, any of the above areas. And that suits me just fine, because I prefer to spend my time pursuing and doing what I enjoy most: writing. I have always enjoyed writing. Even as a kid, I liked to write letters and still do. How many people do you know who sincerely like to write letters? Not many, I'm sure. In fact, some people look at me in a peculiar way when I tell them I do, as if that makes me some sort of weird freak.

In addition to writing letters, I love to write short stories, articles, reports and, most of all, books. Writing this is my labor of love. If I don't have a writing project going, I feel downright antsy, nervous, and vaguely discontented. Remember those "sixty-second advertisements" I mentioned in my personal story? I'm referring to commercials, radio commercials in particular. I even enjoyed writing most of my many commercials during my broadcast years. Guess that does make me a real weirdo!

Throughout my twenty-year broadcast career, I wrote commercials at almost every station I worked for, both radio and television, regardless of my main assignment. Even if I had an on-air position as a talk show host or weather girl, for example, somewhere in the station was a desk I occupied when I wasn't on the air or on camera. And, at every station, I wore an invisible hat that seemed permanently attached to my head that said "Alice Potter, Copywriter."

I wrote thousands of commercials over the years about every subject, product, business, and service imaginable to man. Many areas I knew nothing about and then it was a chore and a drag to pour out approximately 150 words on the subject which, depending on delivery, comes to sixty seconds. Go to any Yellow Pages telephone directory and look at the various categories covered. I guarantee I have written about each and every one at some time or another. Many were not up my alley whatsoever, such as artificial insemination for cattle and overcoming corn worm infestations, both written in the farmlands of South Dakota, but if it was my assignment to write on such subjects, I did it. Can you hear me saying "I can do that"?

My favorite radio commercials were what I call "production spots." These were like mini stories and featured characters, sound effects, and music. Naturally, I wrote myself into each production. Then I, along with the other characters in the production, would assemble in the studio where, with the assistance of an engineer, the commercial would be produced. Our own little theater group! What fun we had! The very best part of all was hearing my spot and my character adaptation later that evening on my car radio

as I drove home from work: instant gratification of the first order. All that was missing was the applause. But I was known to signal other drivers on the freeway and point to my radio, hoping they'd get the message and turn on their car radios. Obviously, they didn't understand and wouldn't have known which station to tune in to, anyway, but I still wanted to share my personal sixty seconds of fame.

Yes, writing is my passion. My talent? I hope so! At least I approach every project with an I-can-do-that attitude and, as with the difficult commercials I encountered, miraculously, the task gets done. Other Alice passions? They'll be revealed sooner or later so, as they say in radio, stay tuned!

Throughout this chapter, I've urged you to recognize and honor your passions and talents. This is no time to be modest or to deny the existence of these important fundamental attributes that burn within you. Everyone has passions; everyone has talents. And you—*especially you*—have passions and talents. Please, think about them and honor them now. We'll explore additional ways to unearth your unique passions and talents in chapter 4. For now, and as I said earlier, remember that you're not expected to do everything, just your *own* thing.

Your "I Can Do" Review

What are your passions? List them here.

_____

_____

_____

_____

What are your talents? List them here.

_____

_____

_____

If you had the time and necessary resources to do or to be anything you wanted, what would that be? Write some of those desires here.

_____

_____

_____

_____

What is, or seems to be, in the way of your following your passions, talents, and desires?

_____

_____

_____

_____

Remember the three easy-action words: *identify, commit,* and *do.* Start now to put them into practice.

Ponder This

Passion is in all great searches and is necessary to all creative endeavors.

—*W. Eugene Smith*

4

Do I Really Want To?

Learning to Discover, Discern, and Evaluate

You have to know what you want to get.

—Gertrude Stein

Are you all charged up now, ready to do it? But what is *it?* Sometimes deciding what it is you want to do is the biggest problem or decision of all. You already know you can't do everything; there's not enough time or money, and you don't have enough energy to, as Mark suggested, climb the highest mountains, sail the distant seas, win the coveted medals, and all the rest of it.

Now is when you are faced with the challenge of discovering the special passions and talents lurking within you, the passions and talents that you, and only you, have to offer, the individual path that you want to take. This can be quite intimidating but also fun. So let's enjoy discovering, discerning, and evaluating what is appropriate for the unique you.

Yes, you are unique; no one else on earth is quite like you, no one else has your particular passions and talents. That is as it should be; otherwise, we'd all aspire to the same things, reach for the same goals. How dull and boring! Everyone would be doing the same things. But who would be doing the other things? And all of it needs to be done in order for us to have a balanced, productive world. That's why we were all created with different interests, passions, and talents. Aren't you glad? I know I am!

One way to determine what really turns you on is to look back over your life and remember some of the things that gave you a feeling of accomplishment, satisfaction, or excitement in years past. It doesn't have to be something monumental; a small, treasured memory will do. Examine it, relive the feeling, and actively experience the emotions you felt at that time. Perhaps a budding talent was trying to push its way through, but you didn't fully recognize it at that time. Look at this memory from every angle; it may be trying to tell you something.

I'll give you an example from my life. When I was in junior high school, in seventh or eighth grade, I enrolled in sewing class. It wasn't that I enjoyed sewing so much but that, by making my own clothes, I had a better chance of increasing my wardrobe. Actually, I turned out to be a decent seamstress and continued to make all of my own and my children's clothes for many years.

The high school put on a big fashion show featuring the girls in the junior high sewing class. As you will recall, as a young person, I felt anonymous and invisible. I was scared to death at the prospect of being in front of an audience. Going out on the stage was a major stretch for me, but it was something that I had to do; I was in the program. On the evening in question, I was trembling and felt close to tears. When my turn came, and I got to the center of the stage with the spotlight focused on me, I did my required number of turns. But something happened to me in that short moment in time. Because I was so scared, rather than breaking down in tears, I found myself smiling like crazy. And then it happened! A brand-new feeling of confidence swept over me. There was some applause and the spotlight felt good. I didn't want to leave. I felt special, recognized, like a new person, a real person—no longer anonymous and invisible. I can relive that exact moment today. I liked

being on stage. I liked being in the spotlight. I liked the applause.

It turned out that a talent scout from a teenage magazine was in the audience. Through the school, the people from the magazine contacted my parents and suggested an audition with the prospect of my becoming a model for the magazine. They said I had such a wonderful smile and great presence on stage. This terrified my mother and the thoughts of any future modeling career were squashed at that moment. "Absolutely not!" was the verdict. Someone, some unknown person was going to take Alice's picture? "Absolutely not!" Alice might appear in a magazine that would be read around the country? "Absolutely not!" Mother was worried enough about me in the ordinary course of life; the thought of "bad things happening" as the result of my exposure in a national magazine was too much for her. She would not even consider exploring the prospect. I am amused at the number of stage-door mothers who, these days, would have given anything for that opportunity. I was absolutely brokenhearted, and I remember that to this day, too. Of course, there was no guarantee that I would have passed the audition and found a future in the teen fashion industry, but the thought of what might have been still haunts me.

Now let's examine this little vignette. In participating in the fashion show, I discovered that I liked being on stage and in the spotlight. I discovered that applause turned me on. I was told I had a great smile and good stage presence. Therefore, throughout the years, I participated in fashion shows whenever I could. Mostly, they were charity events; I never was paid to model. But, on the runway, I always felt the same charge, the same exuberance that I felt that night on stage back in junior high school.

At one time, I answered a classified ad for a model. It turned out the sleazy character that interviewed me had something else in mind, and I beat it—quickly! But, for a long time, I thought I'd really feel fulfilled if I were a model. I was still hurting over my mother's dashing of what, to me, was a dream come true.

Upon recent analysis, I think my short-lived passion for singing came from my desire to recapture that warm and wonderful feeling that being on stage in the spotlight gave me. Perhaps that's why I enjoyed my broadcast career so much. I was in show biz. Even if I were in a studio with just a microphone, some cameras, but no audience, and consequently no applause, I always knew there were people out there somewhere and I was on stage.

But, to explore this vignette even further, I think the reason I enjoy public speaking—which excites me as much as writing—is because speaking gives me the very same charge today that I got all those years ago on stage at Millburn High School. I don't want you to think I'm totally ego driven, I also feel I have much to contribute to audiences in the way of my message, about which I'm very, very serious.

In retrospect, it seems that almost everything I've done in my life that has really turned me on relates to that long-ago, brief, but powerful experience. My short excursion into the world of little theater is another example. A fun involvement, if you share my love of the stage and spotlight. If I had time to do everything I'd like to do, I'd immediately look for the nearest local company and volunteer my services. In fact, I may do that as soon as I'm finished with this manuscript.

What did I learn from my trip through memory lane? I learned that my true passion lies in areas that involve being in front of people: modeling, speaking, acting. Talent? In my case, very little, I expect. Initially, that is. As they say, "Fake it till you make it!" No matter what it is you want to do, if you have a passion for it, you have the ability to succeed at it. That's so important that I'm going to repeat it: *No matter what it is you want to do, if you have a passion for it, you have the ability to succeed at it.*

Why do I say that? Because, if you are passionate about whatever it is you want to do, you are going to work at it. You're going to read up on it. You're going to do it, and do it, and do it some more until you become good at it. You are never going to give up until you are the expert, until you succeed. You are going to heed the words of Winston Churchill who said, "Never give up. Never. Never. Never."

You may have a lot of fears in this area. You may be afraid of giving your best effort because you're afraid of failing. There are probably those out there who've said, "You can't do that," and you don't want to hear them say, gloatingly, "I told you so!" You may even be afraid of succeeding; hypocritical friends often fall by the wayside when one succeeds. But how will you know, if you don't accept the challenge and run with it? Remember, we're talking about something that you care about so strongly, so passionately, that you're not only willing but anxious to go the extra mile, to do whatever it takes.

If you agree, follow my example and pursue the back-to-childhood experience. Now it's your turn to take a trip down memory lane. What are some of the things you enjoyed as a child, young person, or early adult? Skiing, sailing, or skateboarding? How about fishing, hunting, or bird watching? Did you like to work with your hands on cars, with wood, or making a variety of things from jewelry to birdhouses? Did you feel a surge every time you took up a pencil or brush to draw, sketch, or paint? Were you intrigued by cameras, computers, or electronic equipment? Can you reignite that interest today? Is it something you can see yourself doing now, today, possibly in some new or revised form?

No? You went back through your life—all the way to junior high school like I did—and you didn't come up with anything? Okay, we'll look elsewhere. Have you ever leafed through an adult education flyer or college extension brochure? There are all sorts of intriguing courses being offered: exotic cooking classes, foreign languages, flower arranging, interior decorating, and financial courses of every description. You could explore your computer from here to eternity and never really learn its full capabilities. The field of psychology and human relations seems to be expanding daily. What about sales, customer service, marketing, public relations, and promotion? Child rearing and parenting classes are becoming more predominant. The choices are endless. Call up your local school or community college and get on their mailing list. Read over their literature. Something is bound to get your juices flowing. Then, sign up for a short course. You have nothing to lose and everything to gain.

Think about a course you may have taken and enjoyed years ago. Maybe you intended to get back to the subject, but something got in the way, like a marriage or a child or two. It's never too late to start again. Marilyn took a course in interior designing way back when. She loved it and had a real knack for the field of design, but she met a handsome guy, there was a war on, and you know how that goes. She got married and had three children. Some time later, when

the kids were finally all in school, she determined to get back into the field she always loved. She did so and, due to her obvious gift, became much sought after in affluent circles. Marilyn adores designing and all aspects of interior decorating. Talented? You better believe it! I only wish I could afford her services!

Peter, as a child, loved to spend his free time in the kitchen with his mother, perhaps because, with the kitchen stove going, it was the only warm room in the house during the bleak war years in Europe. After his divorce, Peter found out he loved to cook and he had a talent for turning out fabulous dishes. He was never able to explore this area of interest when he was married because his wife wouldn't let him in "her" kitchen. Now he has a kitchen of his own and he's happy as a lark preparing the kinds of dishes his mother used to make. He's thinking about opening his own restaurant soon. "Just something small, maybe seven to ten tables," he says. "I can't think of anything that would please me more than making other people happy with my kind of European home cooking." Peter is passionate about cooking, and he has a talent for it. He will be a success in the restaurant business, if he opens one. If not, he's still a success, because he'll always be doing what he loves: cooking for himself and his friends.

Don was intrigued with computers from the moment they entered the market. He took every course available and also learned by doing and by building, modifying, and repairing various models. Don is now a computer expert of the highest caliber. He teaches at local colleges and has individual students. And, best of all, he helps his friends who run into computer problems that no one else can solve. Don is passionate about computers, and he has a talent that won't stop when it comes to making these fascinating machines—and, thankfully, mine—live up to their full potential.

Stephan used to be a chef but, unlike Peter, he wasn't passionate about the food business. But Stephan had a hobby that really intrigued him. He collected autographs. He started going to shows and galleries and talking with other collectors in his free time. Before long, he started buying, selling, and trading autographs in a small way. Now Stephan has doffed his chef's hat for good and gone into the autograph and collection business full time. He's never been happier despite the long hours and travel that it entails. Stephan loves autographs, he's passionate about the business, and he now makes a very good living at it. "Doing what you love for a living is where it's at," Stephan says, exuberantly. "I'll never go back to the stove!"

What is your hobby? Is it something that you could turn into a real job? Regardless of what your hobby might be, there's likely to be some angle, some way that your hobby could become a vocation-avocation for you. Stephan did it with autographs, Art did it with photography, Peter plans to do it with cooking, and Marilyn is doing it with interior design.

Are you beginning to get the idea of how to discover your talents and passions, some of which may actually be hidden from you? Have some of these examples helped you to determine how to discover, discern, and evaluate what is right for you? Please keep *your* desires in mind, not those of others around you who may have ideas of their own.

I want you to cut to your core desires—you may want to call them needs—and ignore the ''shoulds'' others may bring up. ''You should really think about going into (fill in the blank) because it's the family business. You owe it to us to keep the tradition going.'' The fact that you can't stand the family business means nothing to these advisers. ''You should really think about going into (fill in the blank) because that's where the money is. Why do you keep going off on tangents about (what you really want to do)? That's a quick trip to the poor house!''

One simple way to determine if you're truly passionate, excited, and enthusiastic about a specific goal or area of endeavor is to ask yourself if you'd willingly follow that path even if there was no money in it; if the only compensation was your feeling of pride and satisfaction in working toward and accomplishing the goal. Put some of your goals and desires to that test right now.

Where the money is may not be where you, your passions, and talents truly lead. For now, follow your heart, listen to your inner self, then say to yourself, ''If I want to badly enough, if I feel strongly enough about it, *I can do that!*''

Your "I Can Do" Review

Think over your life, going back to the early years. What are some of the things that turned you on in the past? List them here.

_____

_____

_____

List some of the college or adult education courses that interest you:

_____

_____

_____

What are some of the hobbies and activities that intrigued and interested you in past years?

_____

_____

_____

Go back over your list of passions and desires. Eliminate those that may have been thrust upon you by others who think you should follow a certain path. Pull out the passions

and desires that *you* really want and intend to follow and
list them here.

_____

_____

_____

_____

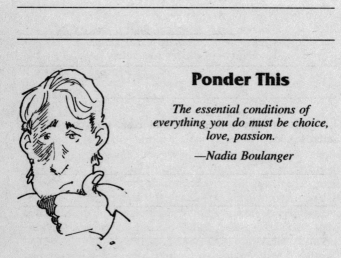

Ponder This

*The essential conditions of
everything you do must be choice,
love, passion.*

—Nadia Boulanger

5

I Tried to Do That and It Didn't Work

Knowing When to Give Up

It is common sense to take a method and try it.
If it fails, admit it frankly and try another.
But above all, try something.

—*Franklin D. Roosevelt*

"Well and good," you say. "You make it sound so easy. Let's get real. Not everything works out. Sometimes, it seems best to give up and move on." You are absolutely right, my friend. I totally agree with you, and I can provide several personal stories that support that point of view.

Years ago, when I was "between assignments," the polite broadcast term for being unemployed, I decided that what I needed was a dynamite résumé and a strikingly different business card. Believing myself to be innovative and creative, I felt certain that I could come up with two eye-catching, attention-getting items. And I did. Because I was attempting to attract broadcasters or those affiliated with the business, I wanted my two items to be broadcast-related. For my business card, I had a miniature FCC broadcaster's license developed; it looked exactly like those we all had to hang in the radio station or TV studio to prove that we were licensed to broadcast. Mine was business card–sized and duplicated my actual license in design and format, including the exact color of the original. I was able to simulate the typeface as well as the decorative border used on

the real thing, making it look amazingly authentic.

For my résumé, I became even more creative. My name is Alice Potter and my initials are AP, obviously. My friend Bill always called me AP; perhaps that's what gave me the idea. AP also stands for Associated Press, the news service with which we're all familiar. The connection between AP, Alice Potter and AP, Associated Press clicked with me, and I determined to do my résumé in the style of the stories carried on the AP news wire that clacked away twenty-four hours a day at virtually every broadcast station nationwide. Somehow, to me, the connection seemed psychically appropriate.

The AP news feed came out of the machine on an endless sheet of ''continuous fold'' beige paper that was about the same quality as that used in newspapers. I was able to get a box of the actual paper and a typewriter that had the same typeface as that used by the AP. Then, all I had to do was translate my résumé into the style and language used by AP in order to simulate an actual story that seemed to have come directly over the wire. It started out like this:

ACP001
   HERE IS THE LATEST NEWS FROM THE AP (ALICE POTTER) PRESS:

(OAKLAND, CA)—BROADCASTER ALICE POTTER SAID TODAY THAT SHE IS AVAILABLE FOR EMPLOYMENT, ASSOCIATION AND/OR CONSULTATION AND RECOMMENDS OFFICIALS OF BROADCAST AND RELATED FACILITIES TO CONTINUE READING.

—AN AP SPECIAL RÉSUMÉ REPORT—

—JOB SUMMARY—TAKE 1

(SAN FRANCISCO, CA)—AS VICE-PRESIDENT AND GENERAL MANAGER OF LINCOLN TELE-VISION, INC. (KTSF-TV), ALICE POTTER SUPER-VISED AND HAD COMPLETE AUTHORITY FOR THE SALES, PROGRAMMING, ENGINEERING AND ADMINISTRATIVE DEPARTMENTS AND STAFFS AS WELL AS ALL OTHER ASPECTS OF THE BUSINESS AND MANAGEMENT OF KTSF-TV. SHE FORMULATED STATION POLICY AND ENSURED THAT IT WAS KNOWN AND CARRIED OUT BY ALL EMPLOYEES. HER POSITION RE-QUIRED KNOWLEDGE OF AND CONSTANT AD-HERENCE TO APPLICABLE RULES AND REGULATIONS OF THE FCC.
12-15-76   05-30-77

—JOB SUMMARY—TAKE 2
   (BERKELEY, CA)—WHEN ALICE POTTER WAS APPOINTED VICE-PRESIDENT, GENERAL

MANAGER AND SALES MANAGER OF KRE AM
& FM AND MEMBER OF THE BOARD OF DIREC-
TORS OF HORIZONS COMMUNICATIONS COR-
PORATION, SHE WAS ONE OF THE FIRST
WOMEN IN BROADCASTING TO ASSUME SUCH
A ROLE IN A MAJOR MARKET. IN ADDITION TO
THE DUTIES AND RESPONSIBILITIES AS OUT-
LINED FOR KTSF-TV, POTTER DEVELOPED AND
IMPLEMENTED ALL SALES, PROMOTIONAL
AND PUBLICITY CAMPAIGNS FOR THE TWO
STATIONS. DESPITE STRICT BUDGETARY LIM-
ITATIONS, SHE ACCOMPLISHED SUCH EFFORTS
BY CREATIVE AND INNOVATIVE MEANS
RATHER THAN BY CASH OUTLAY.

UPON ASSUMING MANAGERSHIP IN FEBRU-
ARY 1974, POTTER DEVELOPED NEW FORMAT
AND STATION POLICIES THAT RESULTED IN AN
IMMEDIATE FINANCIAL TURNAROUND. WITH
SUBSEQUENT INCREASED RATINGS AND LIS-
TENERSHIP, THE STATIONS RAPIDLY BECAME
STRONG CONTENDERS IN THE SAN FRANCISCO
BAY AREA MARKET.

The résumé went on to tell of my other accomplishments
at KRE AM & FM as well as my background and other
exploits in the field of broadcasting throughout my twenty-
year career.

Armed with this new ammunition—my FCC license
lookalike business card and my AP résumé—I headed off
to a national broadcast convention with the hope of making
a job-related connection. I was a bit nervous about visiting
the Associated Press hospitality suite because I was afraid
someone there would take offense at my parody of their
wire copy. I needn't have worried; they were already aware
of the résumé. In fact, the moment I entered the room,
someone grabbed me and said, ''You're Alice Potter, aren't
you? Step inside. The boss is anxious to talk to you!'' I
was ushered into another room in the suite where the boss

sat behind a big desk. His attaché case was open on the desk and he reached into it and took out my résumé! "I've been waiting to meet you, young lady. I want you to know we're all impressed with your innovative résumé. Sit down and let's have a chat."

To make a long story short, I was hired and joined the Associated Press as a BE, or Broadcast Executive, for Northern California and Nevada. Basically, that translated into a sales and PR position. It started out as a dream job: lots of travel, accommodations in the best hotels, a company car, and a substantial expense account. Who could want more? Actually, after a time, I wanted less—less travel, that is. It was necessary for me to be on the road a minimum of five days a week, routinely visiting each and every radio, television, and cable station, as well as all the major newspapers in my territory. Obviously, my job was to sell AP products and services and, for those that already subscribed to AP, to service their accounts and keep the clients happy so they wouldn't switch to other news operations offering similar products in the very competitive market of news broadcasting.

I had just purchased my house prior to the affiliation with AP and, after a year, I became increasingly frustrated with the fact that I seemed never to be able to spend any time in it. Sleeping in my own bed became a big deal for me. The AP powers-that-be wanted me in my car or on a plane from Monday morning through Friday evening weekly. After a while, I reasoned that if I were calling on stations in relatively nearby cities, such as San Jose or Santa Rosa, each about an hour's drive from my Oakland residence, I could stay at home that night, get an early start the next morning, and still produce the same results as if I were starting out from a hotel or motel in one of those cities. I also reasoned that I'd be saving them hotel or motel and breakfast expenses, and I'd get to sleep at home occasionally. That was not satisfactory with them; the deal was I had to actually be on the road.

After a time, I thought to myself, *Alice, you're crazy to*

consider giving up this arrangement. Anyone you know would give their eyeteeth for this job! Why does it frustrate you so to spend most of your nights in deluxe hotels and dine in nice restaurants? Why are you so burned out about jumping on airplanes and renting cars daily? I should add that I was constantly lost driving unfamiliar freeways and country roads. Hotel rooms are lonely; so is having dinner by yourself every night, albeit in a fancy restaurant. The worst part of a traveling job, in my estimation, in addition to being routinely lost, is hanging around at airports due to missed flight connections and while waiting for your lost luggage to show up.

At any rate, after a year, I bid AP adieu and, while I occasionally have regrets when I think of all the perks of that job, overall, I know deep down I was never supposed to be a travelin' gal.

I learned that, when considering a new job, it's important to access your gut reaction. My initial gut reaction to the AP position was that, although it seemed glamorous, a dream job in most people's estimation, it really wasn't appropriate for me. Deep down, I knew I was a home-oriented person; travel, while exciting and fascinating once in a while, could be stressful and overwhelming to me as a regular diet. I had definite reservations when I accepted the position but was swept away with the overall aspect of glamour which intrigued and influenced me and won out over the gut reaction.

Another factor that I almost hesitate mentioning was that of ego. I was elated that my innovative résumé captured the attention of the bigwigs at AP and flattered that they offered me the job. I let that cloud my reasoning and overcome the nudging of my gut reaction when I accepted the position.

Later, I compared this experience with my initial debut into broadcasting when I left what was, to me, a mundane field—that of finance—for the more exciting field of broadcasting. In that move, I had absolutely no reservations whatsoever. My gut reaction to entering broadcasting was,

"Go for it, it feels right in every respect." There were no qualms, no second thoughts, no regrets as was the case with my move to the Associated Press.

Anytime you're faced with a decision of this nature—or any decision, for that matter—go deeply into yourself for advice. Your inner being is all-wise in such situations; give it due consideration. Also, don't be unduly influenced by ego, which can often lead you down undesirable pathways.

Yes, after a year I knew it was time to give up, and I'm not ashamed to say so. My cousin, Bob, took a little longer to request a transfer during his thirty-six-year employment at 3M. This is his story:

"The director of marketing of our division requested that I develop a marketing plan for the division. I worked on this project on and off for most of a year, but my efforts never seemed to satisfy my supervisor. He kept saying that it wasn't just right and to go back and work on it some more. The key element of the plan was a definition of the role that our products played in the marketplace. The end users were mainly in the electrical/electronic O.E.M. industries. Almost one-quarter of a century ago, I determined that the division's products were used to hold, insulate, protect, identify, or encapsulate components sold into the electrical/electronics markets. I continue to read in 3M's annual reports, and my former division and sister divisions still use these very words to describe the role of their products. My failure to satisfy that marketing director time after time was instrumental in my decision to transfer out of that division, after twenty-one years, into our company's international operations."

Bob realized he couldn't fight city hall, so to speak. His supervisor sounds like the type that is never satisfied, regardless of the high quality of work produced. If you find yourself in such a position and you can make a positive move within the company, as Bob did, or move to an equal position elsewhere, it might be something to consider. You've heard it said, "If you can't fight 'em, join 'em." I suggest you add "or move on" to that old maxim. Who needs the daily stress and aggravation brought on by an unreasonable—and often unknowledgeable—boss or supervisor? Just because someone wears a hat that says "The Boss," it doesn't necessarily mean that person is qualified for the position. Have you ever heard of the Peter Principle in which the incompetent are constantly promoted in order to get them out of the way, and they end up at the top of the ladder?

The two situations above are job-related; my friend Hans has a different sort of "I Tried to Do That and It Didn't Work" story. His is a running/bicycling story. Hans, as you may remember, is the marathon runner. A few years ago, after hearing of two women, also marathon runners, who successfully ran across the country from Boston to San Francisco, Hans took on that feat as a challenge. Hans, however, decided to run from New York to San Francisco. He trained for a good six months prior to the start of his cross-country run and, in overdoing squats at the gym, developed a cartilage problem in his knee. Hans was hyped on the trip and he wasn't going to let minor aggravations like injuries to his extremities get in his way. He decided to take a bicycle along, just in case running became too painful; that way, he'd run part of the time and cycle the rest.

Hans got together with my high school friend, Art, the photographer, who agreed to provide his van as the support vehicle. Art would drive and, along the way, take pictures of Hans as well as the surrounding countryside. They departed from Liberty Island, with the Statue of Liberty in the background, and Hans proceeded through Newark, New Jersey, which, I understand, was an experience in itself!

Problems soon became evident in the way of eighteen-wheeler trucks on the highways. Even though the route Hans picked went over secondary roads, so did the trucks, hundreds of them daily, as it turned out. Often there was no shoulder whatsoever; on the cycle that situation was more critical than when he was simply on foot. The trucks, going by at a high rate of speed, created a vacuum that continuously threatened to suck him under the wheels of

the vehicle. By the time they reached Indiana, Hans had had one close call too many and decided to bail out of the rest of the trip. He said, "I decided I'd rather come home vertically on my two feet than horizontally in a box." Hans tried it, it didn't work out, and he knew when to give up. He made a wise, possibly life-saving, choice.

I, too, got carried away at the gym some years ago trying to keep up with the twenty-and thirty-somethings, kids half my age. I have this thing about age. I believe that, once an adult, your chronological age has nothing to do with your abilities. I think that people can be vibrant, fit, attractive, productive, and intelligent on into their upper decades as long as they take care of themselves and are active participants in life.

I have said to many, "Your chronological age is the only thing about yourself that you positively cannot change. It is the only absolute given. You can change your face through plastic surgery, your hair through countless methods, and your weight through diets to reduce or gain. I've heard of instances where height can be reduced through surgery or increased through growth pills. These days, you can even change your sex. But age? You're stuck with it, so you might as well accept yours and get on with making the very best you can of all of your years, especially the one you're in now."

With that philosophy in mind, I became an exercise fanatic, certain that I could turn the clock back and do everything the "youngsters," those twenty-and thirty-somethings, were doing. I participated in daily high-impact aerobic classes in which the participants almost bounced off the walls and ceilings. One day, I landed the wrong way and—you guessed it—I broke my leg! Yes, I tried to do that, and it didn't work. That didn't mean that I gave up. Not at all. It just meant that I had to modify my program, move on to something else. After the leg healed, I continued to exercise but in low-impact aerobics combined with weight training and a daily walk. I knew when to give up on a program that was not only inadvisable for me, but one that was also probably inadvisable for many of the twenty-and thirty-year-olds as well.

We're constantly being inundated with information regarding the benefits of exercise and working out in order to maintain maximum health and prime physical condition. That's all very good advice. But overdoing it, as I tended to do in the above example, can have the opposite effect. Don't ever let yourself get so carried away by anything that might adversely affect your health, physically or mentally, that you put yourself in jeopardy. Know when to cut back, give up, or move on to a different program.

How will you know? One way is to analyze your overall schedule of priorities and activities. Are you living a balanced life, that is, are you giving consideration to all areas of your life? In *The Positive Thinker*, I defined the six areas, or categories, of life as *mental, physical, spiritual, relationships, career-professional*, and *financial*. I emphasized the importance of maintaining balance, that is, investing time, effort, and energy into all categories as equally as possible, versus devoting all of your energies into one or two areas as many people are apt to do.

It's easy, when pursuing your career or climbing the corporate ladder to overdose on the career area while ignoring or neglecting your physical health and relationship categories. We've all heard of stories of the ambitious, hard-driven executive who finally reaches his career goal only to find he's sacrificed his health and family along the way. Or of some athletes who, in their quest to excel, make similar sacrifices, such as those who take steroids, for example. Hans was overdoing it when he worked out to excess at the gym in training for his cross-country run and damaged his knee. I was at fault as well when I hoped to turn back the clock and tried to work out like the twenty-somethings.

One thing to consider when determining whether to give up, cut back, or move on is to analyze your life's balance. Balance in all areas of your life is of vital importance; it's the only way to achieve true, lasting health, happiness, prosperity, and peace of mind.

When faced with a decision about whether to cut back, give up, or move on, ask yourself the following questions:

1. Is my decision liable to affect my mental or physical health and welfare?

2. Could it possibly have adverse effects or cause problems to me or anyone else?

3. Am I considering this based on ego gratification?

4. Will this decision put my life balance out of kilter?

5.   When I contemplate this, what is my gut reaction?

6.   Do I anticipate feelings of regret or failure?

The last question is an important one and can bring up some
unexpected feelings. Regret and failure, while totally different, are both uncomfortable emotions. When we make
choices, there's frequently regret for the choice or choices
passed by for the one we've ultimately settled upon. If you
can figure out a way of having your cake and eating it, too,
you'll probably be able to avoid regret, but for the most
part, we must accept the fact that we can't have everything,
and we usually accept our decisions, often with relief, if
made wisely. Also, there can always be the thought of next
time, another time, or a future time when we can make a
different choice or follow another path if we so choose.

Feelings of failure are something else again; they tend to
be negative, depressing, and debilitating—emotions that
you definitely don't want to harbor. And there is no reason
to. The feeling of failure is a state of mind, and *you* are in
control of your mind. Negative, failure feelings can make
you feel unworthy, and the next thing you know, you're
liable to find yourself headed on a downward spiral. You
may be forced or feel obliged to defer to others in many
instances but, when it comes to how you think and feel
about yourself, no one but you is in charge. You are the
only thinker in your mind. Therefore, you must carefully
guard the thoughts and emotions you let into your mind
about your personal, inner being. Do not let any negativity,
which includes failure thoughts, intrude. They have no purpose other than to upset you and cause you doubts, worry,
and concern. If negative thoughts of this nature arise, call
in some good, solid affirmations. An affirmation is a statement made in the present tense as if the desired result were
an actuality. For negative, failure feelings, I suggest the
following:

I make right decisions at the right time.

I always maintain a positive mental attitude.

Every day in every way I'm getting better and better.

I give thanks for my many blessings. I maintain an attitude of gratitude.

I am perfect just the way I am.

I am a loving, outgoing person, and people treat me with love and respect.

The above are samples only, stated here just to help you get started. Take time now to prepare some positive affirmations that are uniquely suited to you and your situation so you'll have them handy when you need them. Do not underestimate affirmations; they are extremely powerful. Used regularly and consistently, positive affirmations can remove thoughts of failure and unworthiness and replace them with feelings of success and confidence.

Another thing not to underestimate is the lessons learned by your I-tried-to-do-that-and-it-didn't-work experiences. We've all heard it said that we're on this planet to learn, that this life experience is simply a school that we must go through. If that's the case, and who's to argue the point, isn't it wise to heed the lessons learned? Why repeat grades as some of us had to do in regular school? Let your I-tried-to-do-that-and-it-didn't-work experiences, with their wisdom and insight, guide you throughout the rest of your life.

I've told you of some of my personal stories on the subject, and I've passed along some given to me by others, so I think you have the idea by now. It is virtually impossible to do everything and wise is he or she who knows when to give up and move on. I am not ashamed or embarrassed about the times I've given up or moved on, nor are Bob and Hans about their experiences shared here. In all cases, we each learned a valuable lesson and were better off in the long run. The main thing is to make the effort, if it's something you think you want to do, and see where your talent, passion, and desire take you. If, after a while, it doesn't feel right, consider giving up or moving on. Don't make yourself miserable by clinging to something inappropriate for fear of losing face or any other negative that may get in the way of what's ultimately right for you. Remember, this is your life. The choice is—and must be—yours.

Your "I Can Do" Review

List some of the things you've tried to do that didn't work.

_____

_____

_____

In retrospect, why do you think they didn't they work?

_____

_____

_____

What made you decide to change course?

_____

_____

_____

What did you do instead?

_____

_____

_____

What are some of the things you intend to do the next time you're faced with a similar situation?

_____

_____

_____

Ponder This

Here lies one who meant well, tried a little, failed much:
—surely that may be his epitaph of which he need not be ashamed.

—Robert Louis Stevenson

6

I'll Show Them That I Can

Proving Yourself

The greatest pleasure in life is doing what people say you cannot do.

—*Walter Bagehot*

When I tell you some of my personal stories or go back in my life to earlier years, it sometimes seems like I'm telling you about someone I knew rather than someone I was. Perhaps that's because many of these incidents took place such a long time ago, or perhaps it's because I feel that I'm a totally new and different person now. And rightly so. I've heard that our bodies change, cells die and are regularly replaced with new ones, so that we are actually completely different, physiologically, now than we were in the past. Great! Now we're dealing with the all new us! When you look at it that way, it's kind of like starting out with a clean slate, isn't it?

At any rate, looking back over my past life, I think I've spent a good portion of it proving myself—but to whom? To myself? Of course. To others? Which others—family, friends, colleagues? Do they—did they—really care? Perhaps; perhaps not. To the world? Does the world care? Not about me, but there are many well-known personalities out there, politicians, sports figures, radio, TV, and movie stars, and other highly competitive individuals who continually

attract the world's attention. And we watch, riveted to our TV screens, glued to our radios, and slaves to our news-papers, to see what they're up to next.

Well, it's nice to know I'm not alone; many people, the rich, famous, and highly visible, as well as the rest of us, are or have been at one time or another, motivated by the desire to compete or to prove something. Usually the some-thing is that we are as good as, or better—or that we can do something as well as, or better—than the others. This feeling of compulsion to prove can relate to personal mat-ters, job performance, intellectual competence, physical skills, performing talent, and all other areas of competition, and thus life.

There's absolutely nothing wrong with that. Competition is good for us personally, it's good for business in general, and it's definitely good for the many aspects of the world of entertainment, politics, and commerce. Without compe-tition and the need to prove, the sports world, for example, would simply fold up and go away. Has there ever been a sales force anywhere in which the players weren't frothing at the bit to compete with each other or their company's competitors in order to prove themselves? Have you or anyone you know ever competed for the best-looking guy or gal in your school, apartment, or office complex? How about in the job market? Daily, we compete with others as we attempt to prove that we are the best choice for the job, position, or promotion.

Yes, competition and the compulsion to prove yourself is built into your genes just as, in psychologist Abraham Maslov's theory, your desire for shelter, food, love, self-actualization, and all the other needs are built into your consciousness. So, even if you were brought up, as I was, to feel that it's not nice to be competitive because you might offend someone, forget it! ''I'll show you''—or ''them''—can be one of the greatest motivators in the world, as I well know. ''I'll show you, them, or the world'' can propel you out of the ranks of the run-of-the-mill and into the limelight, into a leadership position, or into the big league, whatever that league might be for you.

I do not mean that you must sharpen your fangs and fingernails and ruthlessly go after your competition tooth and nail. I simply mean that you must do your best in any and every situation and, if the situation has particular meaning for you, you should go for it for all you're worth, with no holds barred, not necessarily to prove that you're better, but to prove to yourself that you are capable, talented, and worthy of the goal.

Competition can start at an early age. Recently, in the *San Francisco Chronicle*, I read of a ten-week-long stock market game for students sponsored by a local college. The winner of the competition was a thirteen-year-old seventh grader. Her gain was an astonishing 100 percent! The next best performance came from a team of students with a gain of 91 percent; not bad in anyone's book! The young winner invested an imaginary $100,000 in just one stock; she then doubled her position by opening an imaginary margin account. She referred to magazines such as *Fortune, Forbes*, and *Business Week* to find investment candidates. She got the magazines from an aunt who steered her toward some lists of growth companies. ''I chose the one I thought was most suitable," she said. "It grew for the last four years and made more money every year. Then I looked at the numbers, and I just decided to do it."

The smart young woman felt the risk/reward, based on the stock's history, looked attractive. "She came to me and said, 'Look at that range,' " says her teacher. "She said that it was selling near its low, so it had a lot of room to go up again. Other kids were teasing her because they were going for companies like Microsoft and Intel."

Says the seventh grader, "I just went with my instincts."

Hooray for her! What area do you wager she will be specializing in when she's out in the business world? I believe that she has a passion and a talent for the stock market, don't you?

The interesting thing to me, in this inspiring story, is that this girl is not a one-time wonder. This was the third time she played the game. The first time, while in the sixth grade, she didn't place. In the spring contest, she came in third. She persevered, and she definitely showed her competition what she could do.

This bright seventh grader provides an excellent example of the competitive spirit. She's using competition to grow intellectually, to develop self-confidence, and to increase her deductive and mathematical skills.

I spoke about the high and mighty of show business earlier and alluded to the need of some of our top stars to prove themselves, or to show someone, in order to feel validated. Barbra Streisand, as we all know, is eminently successful in everything she undertakes from singing and acting to directing. But this tough-minded perfectionist has been plagued by insecurities from childhood. In an unauthorized biography by James Spada entitled *Streisand: Her Life*, Spada tells how Barbra has spent most of her life trying to undo the damage done to her as a young girl in Brooklyn when she was called ugly by her stepfather and the kids at school. Her classmates called her "Big Beak" and "Mieskeit," a Yiddish word for ugly person. I can't personally speak for Barbra, but I think much of her perfectionism must come from her need to be better than those nasty school yard kids, to show or prove to them that she can accomplish whatever it is that she puts her mind to.

In a tremendously successful concert tour a few years ago, Streisand wowed the audience, as usual. When her last song was over, and with the cheers of fifteen thousand people reverberating around her, the singer turned to her mother sitting in a wheelchair in the audience and said, "Are you proud of me now, Mama?" Do you get the impression, as I do, that Barbra still feels the need to prove herself to her mother after all of these years and all of her unrivaled successes?

Jerry Lewis, another household name in the field of entertainment, has a similar story. Jerry came from a showbiz family; his father was a star in vaudeville. All his life, Jerry tried to please and impress his father, to no avail. I'm sure you all remember Jerry from the popular and successful comedy team, Martin and Lewis, when he was paired with singer Dean Martin on stage and in the movies. When they split up, Jerry Lewis went on to achieve an equally successful career as a comedian in his own right. After each success and accolade, Jerry would look to his father for validation. But his father always said, "But it's not Broadway, Jerry." To his father, Broadway was the epitome of making it in show business. His father is gone now, and Jerry has starred in *Damn Yankees* on Broadway. Can you hear Jerry Lewis saying to his father—wherever he is— much as Barbra Streisand said to her mother, "Are you proud of me now, Dad?"

My daughter Beverly ruefully remembers her personal showbiz story from her grammar school days. We were stationed at an Air Force base somewhere in rural Georgia and lived on a pecan farm. "Hicksville!" Beverly called it. She felt ostracized and abused because she was the only outsider in the class. Her handwriting or printing was different than the other kids and, most definitely, her speech did not conform. She said things like "can't" instead of "cain't" which brought giggles from the children and crit-

icism from the teacher. In other words, Beverly did not feel like she fit in. For a young person, that can be very difficult.

Christmas was approaching, and the school was planning a Christmas play complete with angels. I made Beverly an angel costume and she was beside herself with excitement over the prospect of being on stage performing the role of an angel. Somehow her being different extended to this aspect of school life as well, and she was told her costume did not fit in with the others because it was made of cheese-cloth. Beverly is a very assertive person today; evidently that trait revealed itself back in the fourth grade. She was not going to be left out of the Christmas play! She was going to show them! Somehow, the main angel became ill, and none of the others knew the lead part. "I can do it," Beverly announced, vowing to show them. At the last minute there was no other choice, and Beverly went on in the role of lead angel, cheesecloth costume notwithstanding, because the show must go on. "I showed them," she told me with gleeful pride as she related the story to me some forty years later!

As long as we're back in the old days, I have an I'll-show-them story to relate from my "former life," which is what I often call the life I used to lead, the person I used to be, and the days I vaguely remember.

I eloped with my high school sweetheart, Campbell, to the consternation of my parents and the amazement of everyone I knew. Invisible, anonymous people do not do such dramatic things! "C'est la guerre," I always said. There was a war on, a big one, and after "Good-bye dear, I'll be back in a year" changed to "the duration," many wondered if the boys marching off to fight would ever come back. To Campbell and me, the obvious thing to do was to get married—for as long or as short a time as was granted us. The response to our impulsive action was much head-shaking and tongue-clucking on the part of relatives and friends. "Those kids will never make a go of it. What do they know about life?" Then, later, when I became pregnant, they said, "What do they know about bringing up a child? They're just children themselves."

True, we didn't know beans about life, marriage, raising kids, keeping house, or any of the rest of it, but I was determined to prove to them that I was the best wife, mother, and housekeeper on the planet. And I went about my challenge with a vengeance! We lived in a lot of funny places during my husband's military career, which was cut short prematurely by an aircraft accident. But no matter what kind of a place we called home during those war years, converted chicken coop, old mining cabin, or house trailer, I endeavored to make it the best, most attractive, comfortable place to live this side of the Mississippi—and that held regardless of which side of the river we were stationed!

I was the epitome of the housewife in the old commercials exclaiming excitedly over the beautiful wax shine on her kitchen floor or end tables. Imagine getting excited about such trivia! I cleaned daily with a frenzy. I never left the house, or whatever our abode, without vacuuming, dusting, washing, and polishing floors daily. Every item in the drawers and the closets was in exact position; I boasted that I could find any item requested blindfolded.

That was the housekeeper part. I was equally industrious when it came to the children. They were spotless and beautifully dressed; Beverly's hair was always newly shampooed and curled and her clothes all handmade by Mommy. I kept Mark so sanitized as an infant that he was never allowed to touch the floor the first few years of his life, although you could have eaten off of those floors, literally. I was an obsessive, perfectionist, neat freak!

Upon reflection, how dumb, how stupid, how exhausting it all was! What a waste of energy! Just think of all I could have accomplished if I'd put those energies to work elsewhere. But I was proving something; I was showing them that their dire predictions were all wrong. I was into proving that, just because I was a very young bride, it didn't mean our marriage was doomed to failure.

These days, when the dust piles up, the silver becomes tarnished, and the dog and cat hairs show on the carpet, I wave it all aside and say, ''It'll get done when I get around to it.'' And it does. And I'm much happier now doing other things that I really enjoy; I don't think I ever really liked all that obsessive housework. But we did have the most squeaky clean, sparkling, shiniest, neatest household in existence, of that I'm certain. So, proving things and showing them usually does end up with some beneficial end result. In my case, it meant an exceptionally neat and clean home and beautifully dressed, well-scrubbed children who looked like they just stepped out of a magazine ad.

My friend of many years, whom I'll call Myra, also married her high school sweetheart when they were both very young. She felt obliged to show good friends who had helped them in difficult times that she was a responsible person who would be accountable for the debts they incurred. Here is Myra's story in her own words:

My husband died suddenly in 1968. He was only fifty years old. We had been married thirty years, so you can see we married very young. We had been high school sweethearts.

The two years prior to his death we had been going through very difficult financial problems. A partnership in business had ended in trouble and forced my husband into bankruptcy.

When his death occurred suddenly with no forewarning of any physical problems, I was left owing a considerable amount of money. Much more than I thought I had the capability of earning enough to pay. But I could not see myself letting some good people down by not trying to repay what we owed. Especially some good friends who had been so kind to help us when we needed help. I decided I was going to repay as much as I could over the next few years.

I was working at the time in a government job which, as most people know, did not pay a big salary. I had a friend in the catering business and she always needed extra help for weekend affairs and some evenings. I helped her when I could. I worked this way for many months and also lived on a very limited budget, trying to save all I could to pay bills.

Also during this time, I decided to go to real estate school at night to obtain my license to sell real estate. At my age, working two jobs, one of which required me to leave home by six A.M. daily, and going to school was not easy. But I

was determined to do it all. I had to get to bed as early as I could. Needless to say, I had very little social life.

After about a year of this, I obtained my license and started working part-time as a real estate salesperson. Since I was getting off my government job at 3 P.M. I was able to work real estate some of each day and every weekend. By this time, I gave up helping my catering friend except when she was in dire need of extra help.

I was moderately successful in those days, and I used all my commission money toward old debts. I finally succeeded in paying back everything that I felt responsible for. This was only done by very hard work, determination, and sacrifices.

My faith in God and believing in doing the right thing sustained me during those times. Also my growing up during the depression days made me appreciate the value of money and hard work.

Myra is a remarkable woman. I met her in the mid-70s after she had gotten her real estate license. In fact, Myra sold me my house, and we've been friends ever since. I knew she was a widow, but I thought she was just working in the real estate field to keep herself busy as many society matrons in my area do. She never told me of the hard times she was going through, but that's Myra; she would never cry on anyone's shoulder. Hearing Myra's story made me feel very proud of her. Not many people would have worked as long and as hard as she did to pay back old debts that her friends might have excused or reduced if she'd asked them to. Myra said to herself, "I can do that!" and she didn't stop until she proved it to her friends. Next time you're thinking about your personal responsibilities, remember Myra and her story.

This chapter, which concerns proving oneself, brings up the competitive spirit within all of us. It's something we're born with. The question is, when is competition good and when can it get out of hand? There is nothing greater than a positive competitive spirit such as that exhibited in school sports, Little League, the Olympic Games, amateur ice skating competitions, and countless other games and contests. There are also professional sports competitions in such diverse areas as baseball, basketball, football, soccer, hockey, golf, tennis, swimming, boxing, wrestling, and more. All of these competitions are, for the most part, healthy and to be encouraged.

But what about competitions that are negative and ultimately destructive? Locally of late, I've read of many sad and tragic stories of dogfights, usually staged by young people in the projects, in which one animal must kill the other in order to win. In this case, the animals—both winners and losers—are unwitting victims. On the human side, competition can get just as ugly; gang and turf wars, for example.

In the name of business competition, with the desire to show the world by stacking up more dollar bills and paper wealth than anyone else, many lose their inner moral compass and commit reprehensible acts, such as bilking friends and colleagues out of huge sums of money in investment or real estate scams, among others. Gullible seniors are frequently prey to unscrupulous predators competing for their limited savings, as are some young people out in the world for the first time, naive widows, and other trusting individuals. Even some salespeople who, early on, would never consider stooping to what might be thought of as taking someone, become, over time, greedy and overzealous in their sales techniques in order to rack up a required sales quota for their company or in the name of competition.

In proving yourself, in showing others, in all of life's competitions, you must be true to yourself, honor yourself, and to be your personal judge and jury whenever in doubt. Of course we know there must be winners and losers in most competitions but, when competing, always consider your methods. Do you care more about winning than playing an honorable game? Did you win fair and square? Are you proud of yourself and your conduct? Aspire to be a positive role model for young people, for those who trust you, and anyone who looks up to you as a winner. Don't ever let them down.

Hans tells the story of a successful businessman who was also a marathon runner. He did well in competition and, to do even better, he hired a personal trainer who coached him totally by phone, never in person. Soon, under the guidance of the telephone trainer, his times became better and better and he became a real contender in his age category. His family, friends, and colleagues were proud and impressed, as was the trainer. He then entered a major race and, as he predicted, he came in first in his category and won a coveted prize. Later, when the race officials checked the televised checkpoints, they noticed that he had missed some. The man had jumped on the subway midway through the race, thereby cutting considerable time off of his overall finish time. Obviously, he was exposed and had to return the prize money. Not only was he embarrassed, humiliated, and shamed, he totally lost all credibility in the eyes of his family, friends, and colleagues, as well as his bewildered trainer who had accepted the man's stories of his fantastic progress as truth.

This is not the first story of that nature that I've heard relating to the field of marathon running. Why do they do it? It's seldom for the money; the man in this story was well off. It seems to be for the prestige, the glory. They're almost always caught sooner or later. Where is the prestige and glory in that?

One guideline to follow when competing in any area is to ask yourself, "Am I hurting anyone, including myself, by my actions?" Of course you want to win, to succeed, to excel, but to do so at the expense of your self-respect and integrity or at the expense of others who might be hurt, ruined, or humiliated is not only dishonorable, it should be absolutely forbidden.

Also, remember the Golden Rule, "Do unto others as you would have them do unto you," when undertaking any action. This rule has stood the test of time; heed it. You can never go wrong when you keep it in the forefront of your mind. Consider, for a moment, the effect on the world if everyone observed this rule, even for a short period of time. Crime and violence would cease; graft, greed, and fraud would come to a halt; the political world, as we know it, would totally change; and hurt feelings would be eliminated. That's just for starters. It would truly be the "kingdom come" for which we routinely petition God in "The Lord's Prayer." I don't anticipate such a miraculous change in human nature any time soon but, in your life and mine, we can observe the rule and thereby affect the lives and happiness of those around us in a positive, rather than negative, manner.

If all else fails, consider the law of karma in which it is said that "what goes around comes around." Why let your past indiscretions influence your future? Let the law of karma act as a stern taskmaster as it reins in any thoughts of inappropriate behavior.

Your "I Can Do" Review

Remember some of your personal I'll-show-them-I-can stories. Note them here.

_____

_____

_____

Do you have issues in your life that, in your opinion, require that you show them or prove yourself? Note them here.

_____

_____

_____

When competing, what are your feelings about winning?

_____

_____

About losing?

_____

_____

List your thoughts about what it takes to be a positive role model.

_____

_____

_____

Ponder This

We prove what we want to prove, and the real difficulty is to know what we want to prove.

—*Emile Auguste Chartier (Alain)*

7

I've Done That

Acknowledging Past Accomplishments

The desire accomplished is sweet to the soul.

—*The Holy Bible: Proverbs*

By now you've thought about some of the things you may want to do—one of these days. You've explored your many doubts, excuses, and delays. You've wondered whether saying "I can do that" means you're obliged to attempt to do absolutely everything. You've started to evaluate some of the things you always thought you wanted to do if you had the time, money, and energy. You've recalled the things you tried that didn't work for one reason or another. And you've remembered with pride the many times you proved yourself.

Do you feel a little worn out after all of that? I don't blame you. Enough is enough. Now is the time to congratulate yourself for all the things that *did* turn out, all the times you proved yourself, and to acknowledge all of your past and present accomplishments, victories, and triumphs. I'll bet there were lots—and there are many more on the horizon. Yes, over the years, I know you've had countless successes in each and every area of your life.

Probably you're saying, as did many of my friends when I quizzed them, "But I haven't done anything. Honestly, I can't think of a single notable thing that I'm proud of; really, I can't.'' Hogwash! Now, to paraphrase Elizabeth Barrett Browning, ''Let us count the ways.''

Are you a housewife? ''Yeah, I'm just a housewife,'' I hear you saying in an apologetic tone. Just a housewife, indeed! Do you truly understand the responsibilities of being ''just a housewife''? You cook and clean and do the laundry. You maintain the budget and pay the bills. You entertain guests and handle family correspondence. You shop for groceries and pick up the dry cleaning. You walk the dog and keep peace with neighbors. Does this sound like the beginning of your job description? If so, you should be darn proud of your accomplishments!

Are you also a mother? In that case, in addition to the above, you clean up messes, kiss skinned knees, and soothe hurt feelings. You quiet colicky infants and cocky adolescents. You're a member of the PTA and you're a Brownie or Scout leader. You cart the kids everywhere—from band practice and piano lessons to the skating rink and tennis court. You sit up nights worrying over your little ones' earaches and your teenager when he's driving the family car and it's past his curfew. Let's acknowledge these accomplishments with pride.

Are you a single parent? A working single parent? In addition to all of the above, you manage to get to your job on time, daily. You maintain an attractive appearance and get along with the boss and your coworkers, even though a few of them tend to be difficult. You wait for the bus or your shared ride in inclement weather, and you spend hours trapped in traffic on bad commute days. You're overworked and underpaid, and tired much of the time. You do the very best job you can, and you count the hours until it's time to go home to the house, the kids, and the rest of your responsibilities. Proud of yourself? You'd better be!

Are you the man of the house? You get to shoulder the major load, at least in traditional families. It's your job to bring home the bacon, romance your wife, and discipline the kids who've been told, ''Just wait until your father gets

home!'' You worry endlessly about stretching your salary to meet the needs of your growing family while saving for your kids' college educations. The way things are going, you realize you'll soon need a larger house with a bigger mortgage in a better neighborhood. Sometimes you take on a second job in order to keep up with the rising costs of everything. You, too, belong to the PTA, volunteer at church, coach Little League, and sometimes you pay alimony and child support to your previous family. You maintain the yard and garden and repair things to the best of your ability when they break down. You're everyone's shoulder to cry on, the one who has all the answers, the man of the house who can fix whatever goes wrong, physically, emotionally, and economically. Isn't it about time that you accept some praise for these accomplishments?

Perhaps you're a student intent on preparing yourself for a successful future. But tuitions have gone up as we all know; your parents, even though they both work, can't foot the bill totally. It's up to you to work your way through college even though, at the moment, it may only be junior or community college. You have a grade average to maintain and that takes many hours of study in addition to classroom time. You've got to do your share, so you work part-time at McDonald's, the service station, or doing yard work and other chores for neighbors. You have a car to maintain, that was the deal when you got it, and you realize your responsibility to that and other perks your parents have allowed you. You manage to keep it all together and still maintain your grades. It's not easy, but you're learning the ways of the world. Congratulate yourself.

Ah, but in addition to being a good father, mother, wife, husband, student, and breadwinner, you've got lots *more* to be proud of.

Are you an artist, writer, musician, or singer? Are you talented in other ways? Does your talent contribute to the pleasure of others? I'm sure that your activities *do* contribute to the enjoyment of others in many ways, even though you may not realize it. Even if you can't think of something specific at this moment, consider this: I'll bet you have been, or can be, a good friend. What about being a good listener? Do you have any idea how many people need a friend or someone to listen to them? Perhaps you like to write letters, as I do. Not many claim that as a virtue, but isn't it wonderful to get a personal letter or cheerful note when your letter box usually exudes nothing more than bills and junk mail? No matter what you do to brighten others' lives, please give yourself accolades for doing it.

It could be that you've found your niche in community service and helping those less fortunate than you. Do you volunteer to help feed the needy on holidays, work with the homeless or the elderly, or counsel disadvantaged young people? Do you do pro bono speaking to community groups and those who need your expertise but are unable to pay? Do you offer your services to charity events to raise funds for good causes? Do you teach Sunday school or volunteer in other ways at your church or place of worship? Give yourself a gold star for these worthy efforts.

Perhaps you have a green thumb and can turn any weed patch into a glorious, growing bit of color. Maybe you can arrange flowers, fold napkins artistically, embroider handkerchiefs, make quilts, or refinish antiques. Could it be that your talents lean toward fixing cars, repairing broken toys,

handling "some assembly required" items with ease, repairing the plumbing or broken light fixtures, and flying kites with the kids? People need people who can do these things. Thank yourself for helping.

Yes, the list of your probable accomplishments goes on and on. Maybe now that I've given you some ideas you'll be able to come up with a list of your unique personal talents and accomplishments. Save them for the end of this chapter.

In the meantime, a big "You Did That" pat on the back from me to you. When I first came to California, I worked at a radio station with the call letters, KPAT. We had a daily feature, a K-PAT on the back to a citizen or listener who was deserving in some way of a giant pat on the back for his or her accomplishments or service to others. Review your accomplishments and then please accept my "You Did That" pat on the back now. You deserve it.

During a recent presentation, Michelle Murphy, an international speaker, seminar leader, and management consultant, included a photocopied print of a palm in her handout material. She instructed us to place the palm print in a visible place in our homes or offices so that we could pat ourselves on the back when we were proud of ourselves after finishing a difficult task or accomplishing something special. I think that's an excellent idea and suggest you make a print of your own palm the next time you go to the copy place. Keep it prominently displayed and then give yourself a personal pat on the back each and every time you deserve one. Or, as she also suggested, you might send a copy of your palm print to a deserving friend or colleague when they've done something that merits recognition. This is an excellent way to get and give positive recognition and appreciation. Try it!

My new friend, Anne, recently underwent major surgery. She was worried, and understandably so, about the outcome and what they were liable to find. She was nervous about the pain she might experience and how she would handle being in the hospital, alone, without the support of family and friends. Anne repeated affirmations that I had sent her prior to her surgery, and she visualized the room she would be in: She wanted to be next to a window, have a cheerful roommate, and pleasant nurses. Her surgery went well and, yes, her bed was next to a window, her roommate was cheerful and, best of all, her nurses, especially one, cheered and encouraged her.

Anne told me over lunch that her surgery was a blessing; it was the turning point in her life. She feels, after being through such an ordeal, that she can handle anything and everything that life sends her way. She said, "I learned so much from this experience. I've become a more spiritual person because of it. I no longer worry about the future because I know that, through my attitude and my perception about my life experiences, I am in charge. I can take care of myself now. I start each day with a blessing that carries me throughout the entire day. Life is wonderful. My whole life is ahead of me and I am filled with joy.'' Anne accomplished a transformation, a turnaround in her life, and her future looks bright indeed. She is to be commended on her new, positive outlook and optimistic approach to what could have been a negative experience.

I first became acquainted with Jay Mulkey when he called me to tell me how much my book, *The Positive Thinker*, helped him. We stayed in touch and recently Jay wrote to me as follows:

> Sometimes the ''I can'' follows a period of great personal upheaval and crises. Years ago, after suffering with panic disorder, a condition characterized by sudden terror, i.e., heart palpitations, hyperventilation, shaking, dizziness, and a feeling of immanent death, I developed a fear of leaving my home and subsequently fell into a state of severe depression. I found myself in a complete state of ennui in the space of one season. Thirty pounds lighter, afraid of swallowing solid food for fear of choking, I found myself literally afraid of walking to the end of the driveway of my home.
>
> As my life situation spiraled downward, I developed insomnia. Night after sleepless night, I turned to one thing for solace: the local Unity Church Dial-A-Prayer. Sometimes I would call up to ten times a night. The prerecorded messages seemed to offer me some hope of a better tomorrow. I made friends by telephone at the church and dreamt of what it would be like to actually attend services. I read a small monthly booklet, *Daily Word*, a compilation of daily meditations published by Unity. In my despondency, roots of hope began to take hold, and I began to read and listen to such positive and uplifting

authors/speakers as Zig Ziglar, Les Brown, and
Jack Boland.

Now, today, some seven years after that difficult and challenging part of my life, I write and
record the prayers for the same church prayer line
that I used to call in those dark days. As I am
recording, it occasionally occurs to me that at one
time, this act would have seemed an utter impossibility for me.

I now enjoy my new friends at the church and
am even being considered for an executive position on the board of directors. As I now travel
freely, I can't help thinking that somehow, somewhere, I may be touching someone else who is
in as much pain as I was. A miracle? It is to me.

Jay has good reason to be proud of himself and his accomplishments!

Linda was born with a congenital heart defect and had
open-heart surgery to correct the problem as a young
woman. Over the years, several other major surgeries were
required. Consequently, she was especially prone to bad
colds, the flu, and anything else that was going around. It
was always understood that she had to take extra special
care of herself. Becoming pregnant, carrying a child, and
delivering one were deemed too dangerous; she and her
husband resigned themselves to being childless. When
Linda became pregnant in her forties, however, there was
no question about what to do. They were going to have this
child! Their beautiful baby girl is happy, healthy, and bright
as a button. The entire family dotes over this miracle child,
as indeed she is. And Mommy and Daddy are as proud as
any parents can be. There can be no greater accomplishment than bringing a healthy, happy child into a welcome,
loving household.

Sometimes, loving households dissolve for one reason or
another and divorce is the only solution. My friend Art, the
photographer, sent me his story:

Back in 1990, my wife of several years and I separated and subsequently were divorced. The reasons for the divorce were, of course, many, and both of us were in part to blame. Perhaps the simplest explanation is that two relatively decent people just did not get along.

During the months after the separation and leading up to the actual divorce, I found myself not exactly depressed but having a feeling of just being down. That was not my normal nature, but the more I thought about the divorce, the more down I became. I even thought that if I didn't do something about it, I might get to be in a fully depressed state.

But how to get out of this downward spiral of emotions? I had the feeling that if I could just get away for awhile—away from all familiar surroundings and friends—it would help. The more I thought about this option, the more sense it made. I felt I needed some form of extended trip, not simply a two- or three-week vacation somewhere. I gradually settled on a three-month time frame as that seemed to feel long enough to accomplish whatever good might come of such a trip.

I had never been away from home for such an extended time, but maybe now was the time to do it. A lengthy trip to a foreign country was not really considered due to my limited finances; a trip in the U.S.A. was about the only alternative. An added benefit was that I would have a wonderful opportunity to indulge my love of photography.

Itineraries of all sorts came to mind. Although I had traveled in many areas of the United States in my job prior to retirement, there were still many that I hadn't seen—particularly the Southeast and the national parks in the West. Gradually, a rough route formed in my mind: down the East Coast to Key West, over to Santa Fe and Arizona, up through the Rockies to the Canadian border, back to Denver, and eventually home.

At this point, reality set in. How much would such a trip cost, and could my limited budget handle it? The first estimate based on a normal method of travel—eating in restaurants, staying in motels, booking sightseeing tours, etc. came to more than I could afford. One option was to abandon the trip. I didn't want to consider that as I felt strongly that an extended trip was just what I needed.

I mentioned my problem to a friend who said, "Why don't you camp out and cook your own meals to avoid the cost of motels and restaurants?" My initial reaction was, "No way!" I spent a year in a tent while in the army during the Korean War and had made a most solemn vow never, ever, to sleep anywhere but in a regular bed with regular sheets in a regular room.

Out of curiosity, I asked my friend about camping costs. He gave me some figures, and I plugged them into my cost estimate. The costs were dramatically reduced; if I were to travel this way, the three-month trip became doable. I might mention that the form of camping was not in a tent alongside the road, but camping in a vehicle in the many campgrounds around the country.

But what about my solemn vow? And did I think I could live out of a vehicle for three months and cook my own meals? I had always been a lover of creature comforts; how would I survive this relatively rough form of living?

I weighed the potential benefits versus my objections and finally said, "If I really want to go on this trip, camping is the only way I can do it." So much for solemn vows!

But as an old sales manager of mine from the South often said, "Goin' to don't get the cotton picked." Many decisions had to be made; many details worked out. Resolving these issues became a labor of love after the initial tough decision to try this mode of travel.

I made the trip in the spring of 1991. I thoroughly enjoyed myself, traveled over 16,000 miles through thirty-one states over ninety-four days, all at a cost of just over $30 per day. I saw and photographed many grand places, learned a lot about our beautiful country, and met many wonderful people who regularly travel this way. Most importantly, the trip acted as a catharsis for what was on my mind and broke the downward spiral of my emotions. In fact, it was all so wonderful that I made another lengthier camping trip in 1993, which included driving the Alaska Highway to and from Alaska.

Art is to be commended for breaking his solemn vow and taking a risk on a totally new lifestyle. He is proud of his accomplishment, delighted with his relatively low financial investment in these adventures of a lifetime, and totally pleased with the photographic results that ensued.

Now, what about you? Have these ideas and examples helped you remember some of your past successes and accomplishments? This might be a good time to review your talents and passions and to recall how they helped propel you into a new activity or adventure, a lifestyle change, or maybe even a job.

Let's also consider some of the personal qualities that contributed to your past sucesses and accomplishments. Are you persistent? Determined? Do you persevere when the going gets tough? Do you go the extra mile when you feel like quitting? These are all achiever qualities; no doubt, some of them contributed to your past successes and accomplishments. Know that you can call on them again and often, when faced with new challenges and changes.

Do you have a sincere desire to help others? Are you thoughtful, compassionate, and tolerant? Do you often willingly put the problems and concerns of others before your own? If so, you are truly to be commended. These traits will go a long way in your future endeavors, whatever they might be.

Acknowledging your past accomplishments is one of the best confidence builders there is. Don't ever underestimate the things you've done, the strides you've made, and the hurdles you've overcome. Don't ever put yourself down because of false pride or embarrassment. Take credit, here and now, for past victories, risks taken, and fears overcome. Forgive yourself for what you may consider failures. Thomas A. Edison, who failed in his first ten thousand or so attempts to create the lightbulb, managed to turn his failure thoughts into a positive one when he declared, "Results! Why, man, I have gotten a lot of results. I know several thousand things that won't work." If everything you did was a success, think of all your missed opportunities to learn something new! Reread that last statement. It's a real thought provoker!

Your "I Can Do" Review

List some of your past and present activities and accomplishments that make you particularly proud:

_____

_____

_____

_____

To what personal qualities do you attribute the above accomplishments?

_____

_____

_____

How do you think these qualities will help you in future endeavors?

_____

_____

_____

List some of the activities and accomplishments you plan to embark on now or in the very near future.

_____

_____

_____

_____

Ponder This

Knowledge may give weight, but accomplishments give luster, and many more people see than weigh.

—*Philip Dormer Stanhope,
Earl of Chesterfield*

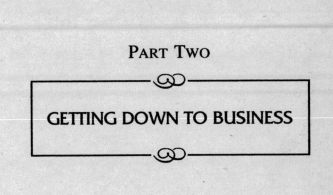

PART TWO

GETTING DOWN TO BUSINESS

8

Writers Write and Speakers Speak

Do What You Say You Want to Do

If you want to be a writer—
stop talking about it and sit down and write!

—*Jackie Collins*

How many times has this happened to you? You're at a social function, a business meeting, conference, or any large gathering of people and someone, to be sociable, asks, "And what do *you* do?" This is after they've told you of their exploits as a rocket scientist or neurosurgeon. Totally intimidated, you search for a glamorous way to depict your mundane job or routine activity. At my age and place in life, I am often tempted to—and frequently do—answer, "As little as possible." I remember how much fun it used to be to be able to intimidate *them* by saying, "I'm a broadcaster," or "I'm in radio and TV!" But my current comment seems to indicate that I'm a total do-nothing now and, as eyes glaze over and the questioner looks around to find a more suitable conversational partner, I sometimes add, "Actually, I write." That usually garners interest as the individual responds, "Oh, you, too? I'm planning to write a novel, mystery, biography (fill in the blank) myself one of these days."

As the conversation unfolds, you find out he/she has been planning to do so for years but is waiting for the appropriate time, place, or ghost writer in order to get started. "But it's going to be a best-seller, I can guarantee that! No one else has a story like mine!"

Yes, everyone has a story or experience in their head that's desperately trying to get out and onto paper. And, as my new acquaintances indicate, all they need is the time, the place and, maybe, a little help to get them started. People who seldom write letters, cringe at having to compose a report, or to prepare anything in writing for the upcoming sales or regional meeting, fancy themselves to be best-selling authors with possible screen rights pending.

I probe a bit and say, "Why don't you get started now?"

"Well, I need a new computer; mine doesn't have enough capacity. And my printer is last year's model. And I probably have to stock up on some new software; things are changing so rapidly in the world of computers. Maybe I'll take a sabbatical and go to Hawaii for three months. Get away from the wife and kids; too many distractions at home. You need the right surroundings and atmosphere, you know. Have to be relaxed, in the mood for thoughts to flow."

Oh, really?

Well, I've been writing for most of my adult life—radio commercials for twenty years as previously mentioned—and, while being relaxed and in the mood helps, it is not always necessary. What *is* necessary is the desire, and/or the requirement, to put words on paper. Often, while feeling rotten and in the worst mood possible, I'd crank out commercials from my typewriter in an endless stream because my job required it and the announcer was sitting there with an outstretched hand waiting for my next piece of copy.

Now, while I write a different kind of material, books in particular, the same discipline applies. I sit in the chair and apply myself to the keyboard. The blank screen, like the blank piece of paper of old, still intimidates me, but I know, sooner or later, the screen or the paper will be filled with words.

This is not to say that writing is easy, by any means. Or,

perhaps it is, if you believe Gene Fowler who said, "Writing is easy. All you do is stare at a blank sheet of paper until drops of blood form on your forehead."

I know the feeling. After I had auditioned for the position of talk show host at KSOO-TV in Sioux Falls, South Dakota, I thought I had the job. But, because hosting the *Party Line* afternoon program was only a portion of the job description, and writing commercial copy was the other, I also had to audition for the copywriter job. I was handed a few facts about a client's business on a piece of paper, assigned to a typewriter in the station hallway, and ordered to write as Mort Henkin, the station owner and manager, looked over my shoulder, waiting for words to immediately appear on the paper. Perhaps imaginary drops of blood were forming on my forehead at that point; I do know the pressure was intense. I must have performed, however, because I was on staff at that station for two years until I left for greener pastures in California.

I usually don't get into my personal stories with aspiring writers I meet at meetings or on the cocktail circuit because they want to talk about their own lofty writing goals. Writing advertising copy seems a very long way away from being on the best-seller list! However, I usually encourage people, if they seem serious, to begin—and to begin now. For most, writing is not easy, but if you have a passion for it, it must be done. Writers write. It is as simple as that. Put your money where your mouth is. If you want to write, write. Waiting for that new computer, software, or printer is simply an excuse. Many famous writers still use the old lined yellow pads and number two pencils to get their words on paper. Others dictate into a tape recorder and, if they choose not to do it themselves, hire someone to transcribe the words onto paper. There really is no excuse not to write if you say you want to write.

If you really want to write, write anything. Writing letters is a good place to start, and it's also a good way to stay in touch with friends and cement relationships. People love to get letters, cards and, especially, handwritten thank you notes. When was the last time you sat down and put your real thoughts on paper for someone you care about? "Oh, I'd rather call. It's so much easier to pick up the phone." Sure it is, but we're talking about writing here. If you want to be a writer, you've got to practice. You've got to write something, and writing letters is a good way to begin. Think of each letter as a mini chapter for a larger book, a column for a newspaper, or a story for a magazine.

Some people like to write in journals, and they do so daily. I advise you to consider starting one. Journals are very private and usually contain thoughts and emotions too personal for the world to see. That's fine. Keep your journal a private affair, but write in it. Write in it every day. Make it a habit. Soon you'll find that you are, in fact, a writer! You want to be published, you say, but you don't have a subject? Okay, look over the material in your journal; no doubt there are all sorts of stories and experiences entered there that can be the beginnings of your novel, autobiography, or series of short stories. Expand on these stories and experiences; flesh them out. There, right under your nose, is an unending source of great material.

Some of the busiest people I know are writers, so don't use the lack of time as an excuse. They dictate into tape recorders for later transcription or use their laptop computers on cross-country flights. If you're a stay-at-home like me, you simply sit down and do it. No excuses. Don't worry about where to begin, just begin. And don't let the desire for a dramatic opening keep you from starting your novel or do-it-yourself book. More people have been stopped before they start because of the need for an opening line. The elusive beginning can be added on later. The idea is to write, type, or dictate—and to do it as often as possible. Anything done on a regular basis becomes a habit. Before you know it, if you get into the habit of writing, you'll soon be champing at the bit in your desire to write, type, or dictate. And it's so rewarding to get those words out of your head and onto the paper!

My friend, Allen Klein, is one of the busy writers to whom I referred earlier. Allen is constantly on planes flying to large cities and small ones all over the nation to deliver his humorous, inspirational speeches. He utilizes a laptop computer and is able to make good use of his long hours in transit by writing in flight, at airports, and in his hotel room. Allen presently has three popular books in the bookstores: *The Healing Power of Humor, Quotations to Cheer You up When the World Is Getting You Down*, and his latest, *Wing Tips*, which is about airline travel. Who better than he to write on that subject? A fourth book is on the way.

I mentioned that Allen is a busy, sought-after professional speaker. We are both members of the National Speakers Association and one of Allen's short pieces was recently included in *Professionally Speaking*, the newsletter for the Northern California Chapter of NSA. I was so touched by his story that I asked Allen if I might pass it along to you. Here is Allen Klein's article, entitled ''The Most Important Speech I Ever Gave.''

When my daughter Sarah was a teenager, she worked at a camp every summer. One year she asked if I would come and do a program for the counselors. I said, ''No.''

It was, after all, a ''freebie'' with no potential clients. In addition, the trip to the campsite and back was over four hours—each way!

In spite of my response, Sarah was persistent. Every summer she would ask if I would come and address the counselors. Every summer I would make some excuse why I could not—my busy schedule, my writing, my fee integrity!

Then at one NSA Winter Workshop, I heard a fellow speaker give a powerful talk. His main theme was how each of us as speakers can make a difference in a discouraging world. At one point, he mentioned that teenagers have the highest suicide rate in the country. I thought about the teenage counselors Sarah asked me to address. I immediately phoned her and asked, ''When would you like me to come and speak?''

After the long drive, I arrived at the camp and tried to find my daughter. She was not around at the time, but from the moment I stepped out of the car, everyone I met knew me. "Hello," they said, "you're Sarah's dad!"

It wasn't until later that I learned that everyone knew who I was because, unbeknownst to me, Sarah had posted hundreds of small signs around the camp with my picture. The headline read, "Do you know this man?"

In my ten-year speaking career, I have never had such great prepublicity. Nor have I ever had such unusual accommodations—a cabin shared with two other counselors, a lumpy cot, holes in the screens, and the bathroom facilities a quarter mile down the road. The accommodations were less than ideal, the food was mediocre and the fee was nil, but the experience was golden.

I could not begin my talk until nearly 11 P.M.— yes, P.M.—after all the campers were put to bed and the counselors had some time for themselves. The room was packed with young, eager but tired faces. They had been working since 6 A.M.

As I started to speak, I scanned the room in search of one counselor that I was concerned about. He was a friend of Sarah's whom I had met previously. He was very shy, and from Sarah's description, frequently severely depressed.

I didn't see him in the crowd and thought to myself that because of his depression, he probably chose not to attend my upbeat program. Then I spotted him peering at me from behind the couch.

The speech went very well, and near midnight it ended with a standing ovation.

I didn't see Sarah's friend until months later. Though he never wanted to chat much in the past, this time he was eager to share something with me.

It seems that several days after my talk, things

weren't going well at camp, so he decided to leave. Since he did not get along well with his dad, he couldn't go home. So he left it up to fate and began hitchhiking. For most of the day, one car after another passed him by. He began to feel more and more depressed and deserted. He started to plan how he would kill himself. Then he put his hand in his pocket and discovered the clown nose he got at my talk. He put it on. Immediately, someone stopped and gave him a ride.

"Maybe lightening up a bit can get me further than I thought," he told me. "Thank you for coming to speak to us—and for changing my life."

I might mention that Allen bills himself as a "jollytologist" and routinely passes out clown noses for his audience members to wear during his presentation. Allen could say the nose he gave the young counselor was "the most important nose I ever gave out"!

Yes, Allen is a marvelous writer, and he is a marvelous speaker as well. As I've previously said in this chapter, writers write. Now I must also say that speakers speak. Throughout the years, I've had the same kinds of conversations with potential speakers as the one I related earlier with a potential writer.

A good speech seems such an easy thing when delivered by a practiced, effective speaker. Consequently, unless they're totally freaked out by the prospect, many people seem to think, sooner or later, that they have what it takes to become a professional—or at least an amateur—speaker. "He was pretty good," says the potential speaker after the applause from a standing ovation dies down. "With a little practice, I could be just as good, maybe even better. It's just that I have a bad memory—but with a few discreet notes to keep me on track, I'd wow 'em!" Maybe so, but what are you doing about it?

Speakers speak. Just as writers must write, speakers *must*

speak. What are you doing about your speaking if that's what you *say* you'd like to do?

"Gee! You mean all you do is get up in front of a bunch of people and *talk?* That sounds easy. And you make *how much?* I'm in the wrong line of work! What do I have to do to get started?"

Speak!

Speakers speak. They don't simply sit around and talk about speaking just as writers don't sit around and talk about writing. Speakers speak and writers write. Sure, writers and speakers *do* talk about their unique professions— to each other and to those seriously dedicated to learning. But they do so in order to learn from each other, mentors, and professionals. Just as with writing, the art of speaking is an ongoing learning process. More and more people are getting into the field of speaking every day, so there's no letting up. The competition is stiffer than it's ever been. No speaker worth his salt can ever begin to think about resting on his laurels.

For a beginner, there are books on the market devoted to these subjects, as well as courses, seminars, and workshops available for the aspiring writer and speaker. In addition, there are many writers' groups and clubs nationwide, plus organizations such as Toastmasters and the National Speakers Association, devoted to helping serious speakers hone their skills.

Buy a book on the subject. Take a class or seminar. Join a writer's group or Toastmasters. Write an article for your office newsletter or a letter to the editor of your newspaper. Volunteer to address your local Rotary or Lions Club. Speak to your church group, your coworkers, or the PTA. Give a pep talk to troubled kids, professionals who've been downsized and need a bit of motivation to go on one more interview, or give a demonstration to your local garden society. Remember, writers write and speakers speak. If you say you want to be one or the other or both, you must do what you say. It's as simple as that!

"Well, you have to have a message, don't you? Something really important to say? I know I've got what it takes, but I'll have to wait until I come up with something profound, a dynamite message, find a special subject. That may take a while. . . ."

Sometimes the best articles and the best speeches are on everyday subjects—thoughts and feelings with which we're all familiar. Another colleague from NSA, Shirley Carolan, a freelance writer and speaker, passed along the following story to me entitled "Jake and Unconditional Love," which she wrote and delivered to a Toastmasters conference.

> When I was a child growing up in England, "unconditional love" in our household was an unknown commodity. I thought I knew what love was, but no one talked about it, much less demonstrated it. I've spent the better part of half a century in my pursuit of it—outside of myself, of course—only to be disillusioned time and again, because love is an "inside job." It's not some happy destination or someone or something "out there."
>
> It's been an education in itself discovering that my physical and emotional boundaries were, at best, very fragile or virtually nonexistent. Today, however, I have a better handle on what it means to be "human." I have the wonderful opportunity to learn firsthand all about unconditional love.
>
> Three and a half years ago, a friend convinced me I needed some male energy in my life. She had three lovely dogs: a black, loving Lhasa apso, a miniature greyhound, and a tenacious pug-terrier. She gave me a choice. There was no competition, I chose the perky, energetic, two-year-old pug. His name is Jake. The lessons this little animal is teaching me are truly astounding! He's teaching me patience, tolerance, respect, especially for his boundaries, which he has a good handle on, and *love*.

I saw that Jake was and is a mischievous little instigator. He got the other two dogs to run away from home with him several times. He was like the Pied Piper. I was struck by his personality and energy. He reminded me of one of my favorite childhood characters, Mr. Toad from *Wind in the Willows* and, of course, myself. I see the same characteristics in him as I see in myself, such as stubbornness and the need to be right.

My friend, Ria, also cautioned me that Jake adores men, likes women, and hates kids. She said he came from a home where he was badly abused. I could identify with that! Apparently, the owners paid $400 for him, expecting a champion pug. As he grew, his hair grew, and they were very upset. Their three little boys did a number on Jake, and to this day he doesn't like children.

Having an animal is a lot of responsibility. It can really tie you down! It's like having a child in the house. The only difference is Jake will never grow up to fix his own meals, clean up after himself, shampoo himself, and so on. But that's where unconditional love enters. I am willing to do these things for him, including taking him for walks twice a day seven days a week, rain or shine, because I love him and I want to provide a happy home for him.

Jake has taught me that he loves me regardless of my moods or how I treat him. He doesn't expect me to be perfect. He accepts me just the way I am. He lets me know by wagging his tail or giving a small bark that he is happy to see me and he usually has no ulterior motives. He really makes me feel connected to the universe.

Jake is a good companion, loves the car, and is a wonderful traveler. Besides getting me out of self-absorption, he's also a great watchdog. He has his own vocabulary, and I know he understands a good deal of mine! He hates it when I do baby talk on him, such as saying "Jakie Poo." He knows the difference between "good boy" and "goodest boy" because he gets rewarded differently. He likes Mr. Jakes and will answer to Willie Woo, Leggies, and Naughty Boy. Ask him sometime.

I realize, however, Jake is limited. When I had an accident a few weeks ago, I thought he'd bark for help when I couldn't get up, or run off as dogs do in the movies, and pull at someone's leg and bring them back to help me. Alas, that didn't happen. The situation reminded me of *Brian's Kids*, an adoption placement show featuring Brian Sussman, the weatherman on Channel 5. The kids are either crack babies or they suffer from their mother's abuse of alcohol while in the womb, or they're brain and/or emotionally damaged. They're all limited or flawed in some way. You may have seen them on TV. Well, Jake just stayed by my side, which is a blessing considering he has no road sense. And so, I know that Jake and I accept each other unconditionally . . . because he is limited and flawed . . . and, ladies and gentlemen . . . so am I!

Shirley won the Toastmasters trophy for this beautiful speech about her dog, "Jake and Unconditional Love."

Explore your life, your family, friends, and job. Surely you can come up with a suitable subject for a speech before your women's club, civic group, or community organization. I was a member of Toastmasters for eight years. We met weekly and I made many speeches, probably close to fifty during that period. All of the material came from my personal life. A few of the speeches—I prefer to call them stories because that's the way I look at my experiences— have made their way into this book or my previous one. In addition, I'm working on a volume of *Alice's Stories*, memoirs from my time on this planet, which I hope to publish someday. I can assure you, there is absolutely no lack of material in any of our lives!

So, if you want to be a writer, write! If you want to be a speaker, speak! Be both; these aspirations fit together like a hand in a glove. Ask Allen Klein and Shirley Carolan or any number of my other writer-speaker friends. Or ask me. We all do both. And we absolutely *love* what we're doing!

The purpose of this chapter and the three that follow is "Do what you *say* you want to do," whatever that might be.

Your "I Can Do" Review:

If you've thought about writing but put it off, list your reasons for delaying.

_____

_____

_____

_____

List some subjects that you'd like to write about.

_____

_____

_____

_____

If you've thought about public speaking but delayed getting started, list your reasons why.

_____

_____

_____

_____

List some subjects you'd like to speak about.

_____

_____

_____

_____

Note resources you plan to utilize in order to get started.

_____

_____

_____

_____

Ponder This

*Life is the fruit of your own
creation.*

—*John Denver*

9

⫘

And Teachers Teach

Personal Stories

A teacher affects eternity;
he can never tell where his influence stops.

—*Henry Brooks Adams*

Next to our parents, teachers probably wield more influence over our lives than any other individuals. Time after time, I've heard the famous and influential from all walks of life give credit to a particular teacher in their past for having faith in their abilities and offering encouragement when things looked bleak. Such a teacher is my good, personal friend, Mona Martineau. As with the quote at the top of this page, Mona will never know where her influence stops in the lives of the students under her tutelage, many of whom may be considered disadvantaged as well as being delinquent, disturbed, and usually disobedient.

Recently, over dinner, Mona told me about her current class. Here, in her own words, is Mona's story:

> When my principal approached me with the prospect of teaching a three-hour class for independent study students this year, I felt overwhelmed. I'm supposed to be retired—actually, I'm working ten hours a week. Did I really want to set up and teach this class each week to kids who have

dropped out or been kicked out of various high schools? They are unmotivated, angry, unhappy, and very hard to deal with. After a lot of thought, I decided, "I can do that!" Maybe I could be helpful in some small way to get these kids back on track and find some success in school.

The good news is that I can and am teaching this class. Not only that, I am enjoying it! The response from the students is very good. We've had more productivity from our students this school year than in past years!

My principal, upon observing and evaluating my teaching skills, gave me the best evaluation that I have had in a twenty-four-year teaching career. At sixty years of age, I feel great! And, yes, I plan to continue doing it!

If, like Mona, you're dedicated to helping others, you might consider some aspect of teaching. I'm not suggesting you give up your present career and immediately head toward college for a teaching degree unless that's in your game plan or goal structure. What I am suggesting is that you can probably teach a skill, craft, or area of expertise in which you have knowledge to others at adult education classes, individual groups you set up yourself, or in seminars and workshops. Teaching of any sort can be fun, rewarding, and exciting—and, as a plus, it can often bring in considerable extra money.

Some years ago, I did some teaching of sorts for a short period of time. I was between assignments and a friend recommended me to a traffic school as an instructor. As you may know if you've ever had a run-in with a traffic officer and gotten a ticket for a moving violation, traffic school is where you must go to—hopefully and sometimes—get the ticket removed from your driving record and out of your insurance file.

I was hired and, after the required training, it was my job to arrive at the college campus where the school was

held every Saturday to conduct class, according to the pre-
scribed manual, for eight hours. This was a traffic school
with a psychological approach as opposed to the usual highway patrol method of emphasizing traffic laws and appropriate driving.

Need I tell you that most of my students were, as were
Mona's, angry and unhappy. Some were also surly and uncooperative—at the start of the day, that is. One of my
duties as teacher was to turn things around; to make them
all happy and cooperative participants, not always an easy
task! Everyone attending had better things they'd rather do
with their precious Saturday; sitting in a classroom with
Alice in charge was not on their preferred agenda.

Nevertheless, they were a captive audience, and it was
up to me to keep things under control. Not that I didn't get
tested, mind you. There was always at least one student
who'd make it clear from the start that he planned to nap
throughout the session, don his shades, lean back in the
chair with arms crossed belligerently across his chest, and
commence to do just that.

Or someone would pull out a package of cigarettes and
light up. That was forbidden, of course. I had to show them
who was boss; it was either behave or leave. If they left,
they wouldn't get another chance at traffic school, and
they'd have to pay the consequences via a stiff fine, increased insurance fees, and have the bad deed inscribed on
their driving record for a very long time. I always made
my point, and I always made it in a very nice way.

As much as I also hated to give up my Saturday to traffic
school, mostly because it commenced so early in the day,
I must say I totally enjoyed the experience. Those who were
most uncooperative in the beginning often turned out to be
the best students by the end of the day. Many classes were
so much fun, we almost hated to part and jokingly spoke
of having class reunions! As I drove home at the end of a
traffic school day, I always felt a great sense of exhilaration.

Richard appeared, initially, to be one of the early-
morning bad guys. He wore black leather and dark shades

behind which he planned to hide; his cigarettes were prominently displayed, as was his in-your-face attitude. *Uh-oh,* I thought. *This guy looks like trouble.* Actually, I had the feeling that he had just gotten out of the local hoosegow. After a few vocal skirmishes, however, he calmed down and really got with the program. As I said, I was being tested. Later, he asked me for a date and, in my best effort at redeeming negative types, I took him to a positive thinking rally. I never saw Richard after that but, for months, I'd come home every once in a while to find a bouquet of flowers at my front door with a card that always said simply, "Thank you. Richard." Yes, teaching has unusual rewards!

What about you? If you genuinely like people and earnestly enjoy helping them, some aspect of teaching may be for you. When? Now!

Fran loved preparing gourmet meals. Her delicious appetizers and entrées, served with well-chosen wines, made an invitation to dinner at her house special and much to be desired. But, after her divorce, entertaining as a single woman seemed uncomfortable; obviously, it was not the same without her usual host by her side. Fran didn't want to give up this enjoyable phase of her life, but how to go about it in a different way? On a lark, she put an ad in the local paper that stated "Gourmet Dining & Wine Appreciation Classes." She was fully booked instantly and, weekly thereafter, welcomed old friends and new acquaintances to her popular in-home classes.

Yes, teaching can take all forms. Do you have a special talent you could share with others?

Rob is a relationship guru. After his divorce, he felt in need of some guidance in that area. Over the past five years, Rob has probably taken every relationship course offered in his area. Now he knows more on the subject than any of his instructors. So much so, in fact, that Rob now regularly conducts relationship classes in his home. Or, if he has a great number signed up for his well-attended classes, he rents a conference room at a local hotel. "Teaching is

my thing,'' he says. ''All my life I've felt I was a natural born teacher. I don't know why it took me so long to realize that and just do it!''

How about you? If you feel teaching is your thing, why wait? Just do it!

Evangaline is a lovely, stately woman of indeterminate age. I run into her regularly at the local coffee shop where she stops in for a cup of herbal tea. When I asked her recently about her obvious good health and vigor, she replied, ''My dear, it's the yoga!'' Because I was considering exploring the benefits of yoga, I inquired where she went for her yoga classes. ''I teach them in my home. Here's my card. You should think about it seriously, my dear. It's the best thing you could do for yourself.''

When it comes to teaching, age does not matter. What would you like to teach?

Jonathon is a publisher and my good friend Marilou's partner in a Santa Cruz publishing group. Jonathon has been in publishing all his adult life and knows every aspect of the business. On the side, he teaches would-be authors everything from "How to Prepare a Book Proposal" to "How to Self-Publish Your Completed Manuscript." He conducts small classes in their Santa Cruz conference room and large groups at well-attended events put on by local and national organizations. For Jonathon, publishing is everything. It's his life, and he enjoys teaching and helping aspiring authors get their books into print.

Teaching possibilities are endless. Explore your world, your interests, and your expertise. Then, place an ad as Fran did. Print your business card as Evangeline did. Put out the word as Rob and Jonathon did. Do it today!

My friend, Fern Barker, whom I mentioned in chapter 3, has many more talents in her repertoire than simply making jewelry. And, in addition to doing, she teaches classes on all of her crafts. Recently, her imaginative mosaic shoe— yes, shoe!—was featured on the front page of the *San Francisco Examiner*, one of that city's most prestigious dailies. I was extremely impressed! The following is part of the accompanying article about Fern, which was enhanced by many delightful photos of her work.

> Fern Barker of Alameda has been teaching classes in pique assiette and memory jars for three years. A professional jeweler for the past twenty years, she became intrigued by a small square of broken tile mosaic she found in the craft shop at the Victoria and Albert Museum in London.
>
> "I brought it home and said, 'I can do that,' but I couldn't," she says. Although Barker had made "the obligatory mosaic table back in the '50s," she found some interesting aesthetic problems in piecing shards together. As she worked

with the materials, she grew to love the method.

"You can't make a mistake," she says. "It's a wonderful antidote to working on jewelry."

After she'd covered half a dozen flower pots, she decided she'd better stop puttering and start peddling. She approached a shop that retailed her jewelry, choosing it because it had convenient parking to limit the schlep. They all sold, and now Barker's business is twofold. Besides the full jewelry line, her pique assiette work includes planters, tabletops, bird houses, picture frames, residential installations and private commissions of all kinds.

"It's a real pull now," Barker says. "Which should I work on?"

Barker buys crockery at garage sales, flea markets and thrift shops and has no compunction about taking a hammer to it. She does have her own code about expenditures. Unless it's really spectacular, 25 cents is tops.

An interesting sidelight to Fern's taking hammer to the crockery: Last week we were both teaching classes for The Learning Annex at a hotel in San Francisco; my course was entitled "Become a Positive Thinker"; Fern's was "Mosaic Art Workshop." Fern arrived with all the required materials, including an assortment of crockery which, when broken, would be incorporated into the various pieces to be made, and a number of hammers. Those registered were also requested to bring crockery and a hammer. Because the floors of the hotel in which the workshop was conducted were carpeted, it was impossible to properly smash the crockery in the workshop room. So Fern and her class adjourned to the sidewalk at the entrance to the hotel where, with hammers in hands, they happily smashed away to the amazement of hotel guests and passersby. Yes, you're liable to see almost anything on the busy streets of San Francisco!

I mentioned The Learning Annex in San Francisco

wherein Fern and I occasionally conduct seminars and workshops. The Annex's eclectic schedule includes classes on every aspect of business, careers, money, and real estate, intimacy and relationships, personal growth, dance, movement, and sports, and all phases of the world of computers, as well as a myriad other interesting and unusual subjects. Most of the people conducting the courses do it on an occasional basis mainly because they enjoy sharing with others, not because the stipend is all that great.

If you have an organization like Learning Annex in your town, you might like to explore becoming involved. If you don't have such an organization, there's always the classified ads, flyers, business cards, and your own living room. Follow Fran's and Evangaline's example; next thing you know, you'll be teaching something helpful, making new friends, and creating a little extra money on the side. You can do that, I guarantee it!

Brendan Lang attended one of my positive thinking classes. Later, he called me to share a personal triumph of his. Brendan was originally from Southern California but moved to San Francisco to care for his uncle who was not well and lived alone in a big house that had been neglected over the years. Brendan who is in construction, set about to fix up the place. He made needed repairs and undertook an extensive renovation plan to increase the value of the property. Brendan soon discovered that his uncle had amassed a considerable estate due to his lifetime of extreme frugality. The uncle had no will or estate plan whatsoever and was content to let the IRS take a major portion in taxes upon his demise simply because he didn't seem to care on one hand and, on the other, was totally ignorant about financial matters of any kind.

Brendan knew nothing about such things, either, but he was determined to learn everything he could in order to protect his uncle's estate. He took every nighttime course available and became an expert on subjects relating to financial planning, taxes, and sheltering assets. Through methods learned at courses given by knowledgeable teachers Brendan has, with his uncle's consent, set up a limited partnership, which he manages, that will protect the estate. As an added benefit, Brendan also learned how to set up a trust that will provide for all the members of his family for their lifetimes. A remarkable achievement!

Brendan told me, "It's a lot of work and time consuming. I never thought I could do something like that, but I did it! I really owe it to the courses I took and the teachers who taught me all I know."

This is a double I-can-do-that story. Brendan is to be admired for his desire and tenacity in learning what he needed to in the field of finance to help his uncle and provide for his family. And the part-time teachers, those who often work for very little in financial compensation but receive untold rewards in seeing eager students like Brendan put their new knowledge to work, deserve tremendous praise.

Teachers teach. Share your knowledge. Make the world a better place. You can do it!

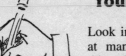

Your "I Can Do" Review

Look into your life. You are an expert at many things. List some of these things here.

_____

_____

_____

_____

_____

Of these things, what would you enjoy sharing most with others? List them here.

_____

_____

_____

_____

Ponder This

*To furnish the means of acquiring knowledge
is the greatest benefit that can be conferred upon mankind.
It prolongs life itself and enlarges the sphere of existence.*

—John Quincy Adams

10

And Singers Sing and Dancers Dance

More Personal Stories

*A musician must make music, an artist must paint,
a poet must write, if he is to be ultimately at peace with
himself.*

—*Abraham Maslow*

I never knew I couldn't sing. Throughout my early childhood, I thought if you wanted to sing, you simply opened your mouth and notes came out just like words did when you opened your mouth to speak.

I found out how wrong I was one day when I was in the seventh grade. The students from all of Millburn High School, grades seven through twelve, were gathered together in assembly, which took place in the school's large theater-like auditorium. We were all belting out something en masse: the national anthem, Christmas carols, or participating in some sort of sing-along. That's when Marilyn Ellwanger leaned across the classmate sitting between us and bellowed for all to hear, "Alice Modersohn, will you shut up. You're flat!"

Who me? I looked around. There was no other Alice Modersohn in sight; it had to be me! I was embarrassed and humiliated beyond words. How awful, disgraceful actually, that I, of all the kids in the assembly, and there must have been a couple of hundred at least, was singled out by Marilyn Ellwanger as a vocal offender! I remembered with chagrin all the belting-out I'd done in the past, in previous assemblies, at parties, and in Sunday school. Just think of it; people had been suffering silently all these years! I wanted to drop through the floor and disappear. I did the obvious thing; I resolved never to sing in front of anyone ever again.

And I didn't. Not until Sioux Falls, South Dakota, that is, and that was by accident. I had taken a job at KSOO-TV where I was a talk show host and weather girl. Bill Cohen, of the Sioux Falls Little Theater Group, approached me to take a part in his upcoming production of *Pajama Game*. I'd never done anything like that before, but it did sound like fun. Knowing it was a musical, and knowing I couldn't sing, I felt obliged to decline; I thanked him for thinking of me. Bill persisted; I think he felt having a local celebrity in his ensemble would be a drawing card. I persisted, too. "I *really* can't sing, Bill, much as I'd like to have a part," I told him wistfully, remembering Marilyn Ellwanger. "Nonsense, Alice," Bill explained patiently. "You don't have to *sing,* all you have to do is yell in tune; it's easy, I do it in all my parts." Thus assured, I became Poopsie, a minor character and member of the *Pajama Game* chorus.

Bill proceeded to try to teach me how to yell in tune. I tried and I yelled, but I couldn't seem to yell in tune. "Amazing!" Bill exclaimed. You're the first person in all my little theater days who can't do it! Well, don't sing, don't even *try* to sing, *please*. During the chorus numbers, just lip sync the words and no one will ever know the difference."

That's the way it went all throughout rehearsals. Then came the final dress rehearsal the night before our grand opening. There was a full orchestra, and we were all in costume. Everything went well until the cast and chorus, Poopsie included, started singing the theme, "The Pajama Game is the game I'm in and I'm proud to be in the Pajama Game . . . I love it! Every day I wake and rush to get to

work at eight. Nothing's quite the same as the Pajama Game!''

Suddenly Bill shouted, ''Stop the music, stop the music. Damn it, Alice, are you singing? Didn't I tell you to lip sync only? Now, shut up and let's get on with it. This is our last rehearsal, remember; everything must be perfect. Music, please.'' And the orchestra resumed while the old humiliating feelings washed over me once again. Furious with myself, I railed, *How did I let that happen?* Obviously I had gotten so carried away with the spirit of the production that, when I opened my mouth to lip sync, the words just spilled out. Now it became a solemn vow; I will never, ever, under any circumstances, sing out loud again!

Being Poopsie was fun, great fun. Don't you just love that name? It went especially well with Potter and, for months after *Pajama Game* was history in Sioux Falls, mail came to me at the TV station addressed to Poopsie Potter!

After I moved to California, I decided to take a battery of aptitude tests. The tests were available to me through the Veterans Administration, so why not? Maybe my real talents lay in a totally different direction, I thought, not really wanting to give up broadcasting, but thinking about what was best for the rest of my life. In addition, I was curious. The tests took two full days; on the third, I returned for the evaluation. What I learned floored me. According to the tests, I supposedly had the desire and ability to be a lawyer on one hand; on the other, my reading went off the chart in the area of becoming a vocalist! Who, me, a lawyer? You've got to be crazy! And as far as my being a vocalist, perhaps the folks administering the tests ought to confer with Marilyn Ellwanger and Bill Cohen. So much for aptitude tests! I might add that my son, Mark, is an attorney. Could it be the genes?

Singing, or trying to, did not become an issue in my life again for a number of years. Then, once again, it snuck in while on a visit to Dad in New Jersey. Dad was mourning Mother's passing; she'd died some months before, and Hans and I took him out to dinner at one of my favorite New Jersey restaurants, the William Pitt, to try to cheer him up. After our early meal, I couldn't bear the thought of going back to Dad's apartment, so I said, "It's so comfortable here, why don't we hang around awhile, have another drink, and talk." Soon we noticed a great deal of activity in the restaurant; the place began to fill up. A stage at one end of the room was illuminated, and a man started playing piano. Other musicians arrived as did a group of senior citizen types, all singers; great singers, it turned out. Most were retired professionals.

For the first time since Mother's death, Dad smiled. In fact, he laughed and applauded. His appreciation was so sincere that, after the performance, the singers were drawn to him like a magnet. One by one, they introduced themselves to Dad, and they each invited him to return. It turned out that this was a regular Saturday night occurrence at the William Pitt. They also elicited a promise from Hans and me that we would return on our next visit to New Jersey and sing for them!

Well, a promise is a promise. I had to do something about that. Somewhere there must be someone who could teach me to sing some sort of ditty to get me off the hook, I thought. That's when, quite by accident, I heard about Betty Link. Betty conducted a singing class in San Francisco. Her guarantee was that she could teach even the worst singing-impaired individual to sing. I would be her biggest challenge!

I contacted Betty and she was excited by the challenge I threw her. But, she said, her next class was to be followed by KTVU-TV, Channel 2, because their top news anchor, Elaine Corral, would be in the class. If TV made me nervous, perhaps I should opt for a subsequent class. Me, nervous about TV? Are you kidding? That was all the incentive I needed. "Sign me up," I told Betty excitedly. "Where and when is the first class?"

Betty gave me her address and time of the upcoming class. "Oh, and bring a jug of wine," she ordered. "You'll need to get loose!" *A woman after my own heart,* I thought. *This is going to be fun!*

Hans and I arrived, wine jugs in hand. Elaine and her Channel 2 TV crew, as well as some other San Francisco big names, including a leading newspaper entertainment critic, were already there. I poured a generous glass of wine; best I get loose in a hurry for this!

Elaine had a good voice, as did most of the others. Even Hans surprised me; I'd never heard him sing before. Betty's reaction to my voice was the same as Marilyn Ellwanger's and Bill Cohen's. "Not to worry, Alice," she assured me. "I've never had a student I couldn't teach. You need just the right piece. Don't give up, I'll find it for you."

Class progressed. Students were assigned numbers to perform. Each week, Betty brought something new for Alice to try. No luck. Then, like Bill, she decided that I should try to speak, rather than sing, in tune. But, in addition to being flat, I can't carry a tune; wasn't that the problem from the start? Speaking in tune simply wouldn't work, either. Well, time was running out. It was almost time for our graduation ceremony, which was to take place at one of San Francisco's leading nightclubs, a tradition with all of Betty's classes. At her urging, one of Betty's friends wrote an original story for me. It reminded me of an old, rather sick joke I'd heard when I was a kid. It was about a gal who gets picked up in a bar and, when she and her new man go to the motel, she starts removing things: her wig, her false teeth, her fake eye. Disgusting. But it was my assignment; we'd run out of time.

We rehearsed in Betty's apartment. Hans sang "Mack the Knife" in German, the others sang their assigned songs, and Alice told her story in the best talk-tune she could muster. All the while, the TV cameras were grinding away, capturing the whole scene for posterity.

Ah yes, we did appear at the nightclub. We all performed. I was glad that Betty advocated getting loose before hitting the stage; it was the only thing that saved me. We brought down the house. Having given up all hopes of becoming a professional singer, I wondered if I might have a career as a stand-up comic; definitely the audience laughed at me.

But what about all the footage taken by Channel 2? It appeared on their famed *Segment Two* program, not only once but several times. In fact, they have reruns at off times every year or so, and occasionally someone will stop me on the street to say they saw me "singing" at 2 A.M. or some other ungodly hour. One evening, Hans and I went to one of our favorite San Francisco restaurants, the Washington Square Bar and Grill, and a man rushed up to us as we entered while exclaiming excitedly to the crowd, "The singers, everyone! The singers are here!"

Somewhat flushed with our "success," Hans and I still had our appearance at New Jersey's William Pitt to contend with. A promise is a promise, after all, but I wasn't going to expose them to the off-color ditty Betty assigned me. I had to come up with something appropriate, something that would make Dad proud. What other than "My Heart Belongs to Daddy"? I bought a Marilyn Monroe rendition of the song on record and listened a couple of hundred times, or so it seemed. In breathy Marilyn Monroe fashion, I whispered the lyrics into the microphone. Whispering, albeit off key, was far better than my singing approaches of the past. I think I pulled off a haphazard imitation; at least Dad enjoyed it, and I paid off my obligation to the William Pitt singers.

An interesting sideline to my singing story is Dad's. After becoming a regular member of the audience at the William Pitt Saturday night singing fests, the singers invited Dad to join them on stage. Or maybe he asked them if he could. Whatever, in his late eighties, Dad became a singer! And he was good! His signature song was "Me and My Shadow." Eventually, he had a real live shadow in the form of Martha Lee, his new lady friend, who enjoyed performing that number along with Dad.

During one of our weekly telephone conversations, Dad informed me that he thought it was time to expand his repertoire. He asked how I felt about "Tea for Two." He then proceeded to sing the number for me over the phone, with little "doo be doos" thrown in every so often. The "doo be doos" represented the soft shoe number that he planned to execute along with his rendition of the song. It was absolutely delightful! Now, Dad had an encore number when audience members shouted, "More, Gus, give us more!" My Dad had turned into George Burns! The incredible thing about Dad's entrance into showbiz is that, of all people on the face of this earth, Dad is the last one anyone would have expected to get up in front of an audience and perform, especially to sing and dance. Dad was a banker, having spent fifty years in Newark's oldest financial institution and, as such, he exuded the stern, rather humorless persona befitting a lifelong member of that profession. Behind that gruff exterior lurked a singer and dan-

cer yearning to get out. Do you have one inside of you?
Don't keep him captive. Do something about it!

I am convinced Dad's renewed interest in life, brought
on mostly by his venture into singing and soft shoe, and a
bit by Martha Lee, extended his life a number of years.
Definitely, his quality of life was vastly improved through
this new, totally unexpected, avenue.

Yes, there is hope for all of us. Life should never be
boring or mundane. Who knows what's liable to turn up,
what new adventures lie ahead, what new areas there are
to be explored. The important thing is to go for it. If, like
me, singing is something you think you might like to try,
just do it. Chances are you'll have a ball! Dad was in his
late eighties when he started; what are you waiting for?

As for my future singing plans? I'll continue to lip sync,
thank you. People seem to prefer it that way. But, if you'd
like a Marilyn Monroe imitator to perform at your next
event, call me. I might be able to arrange it.

Singing, except for solemn operas and some plaintive
country western songs, is overall, a happy activity. Remember Gene Kelly's marvelous song and dance rendition of
"Singing in the Rain"? Watching a news clip of his magnificent performance, as I did recently, never fails to raise
my spirits. I challenge you to watch that with a frown on
your face! Rose, who does housework for me, is one of the
happiest people I know. The entire time she is in my home,
Rose sings. Housework never, ever put me in the mood to
sing, but we're all different. Evidently, Rose enjoys it, and
it's a definite pleasure to have her around; she invariably
brightens my day with her humming, singing, and genuinely happy smile.

Right now, why don't you hum a happy tune and
brighten up your day? If you've always harbored a hidden
desire to sing, now's the time to begin. Find someone like
Betty Link and take lessons. Since most people really *can*
carry a tune, you'll probably be starting off far ahead of
where I began. Or join a group, a barbershop quartet, perhaps, or your church choir. Many of today's top vocalists

found their start singing gospel songs in church. Buy a sing-along tape and belt out to your heart's content. Turn to the old reliable shower. Don't most people debut there? Singing can lighten your heart, enrich your soul, and uplift your spirits. If all else fails, drop in at your local pub where you're liable to find a piano bar. Everyone's given an equal chance to sing at such places and the versatile piano players can usually make most people sound far better than they really are. Go on, cast aside those inhibitions and have a blast!

Dancing, like singing, is equally good for the psyche. Common to all of us is the inbred desire to move to music. If you don't believe me, just watch little children. And the move-to-music thing is ageless and boundless. People of every culture, on every inch of the globe, civilized and semicivilized, in cities as well as jungles, move to music.

Gene was one of the first people I meet when I first moved to California. We became good friends and did almost everything together. Frequently, when we'd be shopping for groceries or standing in line at the movie theater, a little old lady type would rush up to Gene and tell him how much she missed being with him on the dance floor. After this happened several times, I asked Gene what was with him and these older women.

It turns out Gene had been an Arthur Murray dance instructor for a number of years. Evidently, during that period, these senior ladies continued to sign up for additional classes just to be able to dance with Gene. I thought, *I must experience this firsthand,* so, some months later when we were invited to a large wedding, I was ready for the Gene phenomenon. The wedding reception was held in a large hall with a mammoth dance floor. There was a live band that was prepared to play every type of music requested.

Up until then, I considered myself to be a fairly decent dancer. As a very young girl vacationing with my family in the Poconos, Dad and I won a waltz contest, which thrilled me to pieces. Years later, my friend Al Cahill and I won a twist contest held in the resort hotel in the Adi-

rondacks where Marjorie Morningstar was filmed. Unlike my dismal failure as a singer, people usually complimented me on my dancing ability. That was before Gene, dancer extraordinaire.

The wedding reception I mentioned was the perfect place for us to experiment with a variety of dances. Gene escorted me onto the floor; the first number was a waltz. Good, I was on familiar ground. But waltzing with Gene was not the same as waltzing with Dad! As soon as we began, I felt that Gene and I could have made Astaire and Rodgers look like amateurs. But it wasn't anything I did, it was all in Gene's lead. Next came a tango. I would never have dared to attempt the tango, but Gene said not to worry; he'd take me through it. And so he did. To this day, I can't imagine how he managed to guide me through this complicated dance that I'd never even tried before. Halfway through the number, I noticed that the floor had cleared; we were dancing solo. And then, the applause! It was like that with every other number thereafter: polka, swing, rumba, fox-trot; Gene was a master of them all.

It was then that I understood the magic that dancing can bring into your life. No wonder the grandmothers of the East Bay adored Gene! He made them feel young again as he guided them around the floor. He made them look good and feel ageless. For as long as the music lasted, Gene was Prince Charming; he had the ability to make time stand still and their dreams come true.

In addition, dancing can be therapeutic. It's good for you and it's great exercise. You don't have to be a grandmotherly type like Gene's fans to sign up for dance lessons; people of all ages find tremendous enjoyment in moving to music. Monika, the mother of four little ones, felt the need of a little excitement in her life. Basically, she just wanted to get out of the house. She started taking lessons in ballroom dance and, because she had such an innate ability, Monika soon found herself beautifully costumed, dancing professionally in elegant revues. She may have a brood of kids, but Monika no longer feels she's just a housewife and mother. Now she has an inner glow and exudes glamour. Dancing changed her life. What about you? Would you like to add a little spice to your life? Consider taking up dance.

Even though, at the reception I mentioned, Gene and I whirled around a large floor as did Astaire and Rogers in their movie routines, space isn't that important. And neither is a partner. You can dance at home all by yourself in just a few feet of space. Don't laugh, I do it all the time. Certain kinds of music just turn me on and I have to move in time. So I do it. Sure, the fly on the wall probably has a big laugh, but I don't care what he thinks!

Brenda decided tap dancing was her thing. It was something she could do by herself without the need of a partner. "It was great fun, and I feel a lot more graceful than I used to, more coordinated," Brenda said. Unlike Monika, she never ended up dancing professionally, but Brenda tells me tapping had an unexpected benefit. She shed the eight stubborn pounds she'd been working on for years.

Ronald, an old friend from the East, just wrote me that he's started taking lessons in ballroom dancing. This was a surprise to me, in a way, because I'd always considered Ronald to be a very serious fellow indeed, as was Dad. He didn't seem the type to indulge in dancing lessons. But he's enjoying it tremendously. "Greatest new thing I've done for myself in years," he told me.

Do something new for yourself. Start to dance. Do it formally through lessons or informally with friends at your local dance emporium. It's not always necessary to have a formal partner, although I notice that many people advertise in the classifieds for dance partners. These days, people can be seen dancing in twosomes or in groups. Or dance solo in your living room. Just turn on the music and let yourself go! As Noel Coward said, "Dance, dance, dance, little lady! Dance, dance, dance, little lady! Leave tomorrow behind." Sam Whiting, in the *San Francisco Chronicle*, wrote, "Dancing is the ideal San Francisco sport. It is independent of weather, requires no fancy equipment or skill, is inexpensive (unless you develop a serious addiction) and is legitimate exercise.'' What are you waiting for? Go for it!

Yes, sing, dance and, above all, *enjoy!* Don't worry what people might think or say. This is your life. Do what *you* want. If you have always wanted to sing, sing! If you've always wanted to dance, dance! Begin *now*. And a one, and a two . . .

Your "I Can Do" Review

If you've ever had the desire to sing, list those times here.

_____

_____

_____

_____

What can you do to bring song into your life? List some ideas here.

_____

_____

_____

_____

If you, too, love to move to music, note here what you're doing or plan to do about it.

_____

_____

_____

_____

Ponder This

When in doubt, make a fool of yourself.
There is a microscopically thin line between being brilliantly creative and acting like the most gigantic idiot on earth.
So, what the hell, leap.

—Cynthia Heimel

11

Runners Run, Walkers Walk, and Golfers Golf

Some More Personal Stories

Decide what you want, decide what you're willing to exchange for it. Establish your priorities and go to work.

—*H. L. Hunt*

I live with a runner. Hans wasn't a runner when I first met him; in fact, at that time, if someone would have told him that he'd become a serious runner, Hans probably would have laughed his head off. It started innocently enough; we went to a Zig Ziglar presentation in Sacramento in May 1985. Zig Ziglar, as you probably know, is one of the world's great motivational speakers and writers. In his talk, Zig mentioned that at one time he was considerably overweight and he felt compelled to do something about it because he had stated in an upcoming book that he weighed 165. Not wanting to deviate from the truth, Zig was obliged to lose the weight before the book came out, so he took up running as a quick solution. He told how, in the beginning, he ran from mailbox to mailbox and telephone pole to telephone pole until he finally managed to go some distance without collapsing. And, yes, through regular running he did get down to his purported weight of 165 and, from Zig's present trim appearance, he has obviously stayed there. I understand that running continues to be a part of his regular fitness regimen.

Hans was impressed. Hans had battled a weight problem off and on all his life, and the idea of running seemed to be the answer. The very next day after hearing Zig, he started running and ran daily without fail for fifty-six days. By then, he was bitten with the running bug. He loves it; evidently the runner's high you hear about does occur and, as hoped, the excess weight did drop off.

Now, more than ten years later, Hans has completed twenty-five marathons; two of them with hairline fractures of the leg. He's had arthroscopic knee surgery and numerous leg and foot injuries and other running-induced problems, yet he keeps on running. When he took early retirement from his government position, he jokingly told friends, ''When work gets in the way of running, there's only one thing to do. Quit work!''

In 1992, he started out on the dream trip of his life, a four-month-long, 3,000-plus-mile run across America after hearing about two fantastic women who did just that. His ''I tried to do that and it didn't work'' story was told in chapter 5. I mention it again to let you know that with Hans, running is not only a major part of his life, it's serious business, albeit to him, fun.

Perhaps running, jogging, or some other high-intensity sports activity is on your list of things that you'd like to do someday. Why *someday?* Why not *today*—or tomorrow, latest? Hans listened to Zig Ziglar, got turned on, and started running the very next day. Watching Hans's transformation was as inspiring to me as it was to him. Obviously, losing weight can make anyone look better quickly, but there was more to it than that. In addition to the pounds, Hans dropped ten years in his appearance; he looks great in his clothes, and he's definitely developed sex appeal! That alone should be incentive to anyone to begin some sort of regular exercise routine!

That may have been part of Annabel Marsh's reason for running but, if so, she didn't mention it when we talked a few days ago. Annabel started running in 1970 when she was forty-seven years old. When I asked her why, she told me that, back then, she regularly walked the three miles home from work in her "tennies." "There were no such things as running shoes in those days," Annabel laughed. She had read something by Kenneth Cooper about being physically fit for life, and thought, *Why don't I just run home every day instead of walking?*

That started an entirely new lifestyle for Annabel. Like Zig and Hans, she became hooked on running. In 1984, Annabel and her friend, Caroline Merrill, decided to run across America. Yes, you read me right, they decided to *run across America!* These two indomitable women began this monumental trip in Boston in April 1984 and, four months later, in August, crossed the Golden Gate Bridge in San Francisco. If you figure it out, this boils down to running more than a marathon every single day for four full months! Can you believe that?

Somewhere along the line, Annabel decided she would run 100 marathons, and she committed herself to that goal. At the time of our conversation, she had completed ninety-eight, having just two more to go. By the time you read this, Annabel will have accomplished her goal. Significantly, her hundredth marathon will be the San Francisco Marathon in 1996. Annabel will be seventy-three years old!

"I'll never stop running as long as I live," Annabel confided. "Maybe I'll cut back to one or two a year; previously, I'd been doing six or seven—sometimes even eight or nine marathons a year."

When I asked her what she had in mind to take up the slack, she replied enthusiastically, "Acting! I'm taking acting lessons. It's exciting—and so much fun! It's a lot of work, but I really enjoy it. I'm the oldest one in the group, of course. I just love those young kids; they're just great to work with."

Annabel is a determined woman who sets her goals and then achieves them. First, it was her run across America, then the running of 100 marathons. It will be interesting to watch Annabel's progress as she continues to set and achieve new and exciting goals in her life.

What are your goals? Right now, think of one, and then, like Annabel, make a commitment to achieving it. If you can do those two things, determine the goal and then make the commitment, you're more than halfway there. Persistence and perseverance will take you the rest of the way to the realization of your goal.

Another woman who is living proof of that is Linda Somers of Oakland. Linda, like Annabel, is a runner. Linda is an attorney by trade but a runner by preference. "Running sort of grabbed a hold of me," she told Joan Ryan in the *San Francisco Chronicle*. "I was good at it, and all of a sudden it was taking me places I had never really decided to go." Like Hans and so many other marathon runners, Linda battled knee problems and pain much of the time. She qualified for the Olympic Trials at the end of 1991 but didn't take it seriously. But the next year, she won the Chicago Marathon and that changed everything. She won the national championships in 1993 and 1994, finishing first in '94. "I came to a crossroads," she told Ryan. "I knew '96 was my last shot at the Olympics." She quit work to follow that goal, supporting herself on savings and a sponsorship from a leading sports shoe manufacturer.

Her knee and other health problems continued to plague her, and she tried acupuncture, physical therapy, and cortisone shots. When she finished eleventh at the Boston Marathon, she went directly to a surgeon and was operated on two days later. She resumed running within days and ran in the world championships three months later. She was the top American, finishing seventh overall. "Then I knew I could make the Olympic team. Ever since then, since August of last year, that's what I've been shooting for. I've been training for it, thinking about it, visualizing it."

Says Ryan, "Making the Olympics, for an athlete like Somers, becomes personal. It becomes not a contest against a course or an opponent but against the part of her that, over the years, wanted to take the day off, sleep in, skip the intervals, scale back on the 100 miles she runs every week." Somers summed it up, "I went out on a limb and set a goal and attained it. This is something that took a tremendous amount of strength for someone like me who likes control and security. In that regard alone, no matter what else happens, it's a victory."

Victories come in all sizes, but whether mammoth or minute, every victory is to be savored and enjoyed to the hilt. Start gathering your victories now. Let them fill you with confidence and brighten your days. The encouraging thing is that victories beget victories; each one you achieve makes the next one easier.

Making the local high-school golf team is far removed from making the U.S. Olympic running team but, for a fourteen-year-old, it's probably the next best thing. My good friend and old radio pal, Dick Fitzmaurice, faxed me the following golf story:

> I started playing golf with my dad when I was seven. By age ten, I was good enough to avoid total embarrassment on the course, but it just wasn't that important to me. It was fun, but it would never replace baseball. Then I turned fourteen.
>
> It was the summer between eighth grade and high school. A new guy I met in English class a few months earlier also played golf. At the pool one afternoon he announced he was going to try out for the golf team the next spring and asked if I planned to do the same.
>
> Suddenly, playing varsity golf sounded like a good idea. But my score cards suggested rather strongly that the chances of making the team were slim. Could I do it?
>
> I started bugging my mom to take me to the course. I started practicing. I improved but not very much. Doubts started creeping in. It was September. School started. I played thirty-six holes of golf every Saturday—Sunday, too, if I could get a ride. I was getting a little better but

still wasn't matching the scores I heard the guys on the team shot. Could I shave twelve strokes in six months?

Then came the ninth hole on a crisp fall day in October. Par 5, 512 yards. Okay drive. Bad second shot. Third shot still required a 3 wood. That third shot . . . well, the swing was perfect. It felt as if I were swinging in slow motion. Grip, firm but not tense. Backswing, straight back. Position at the top, perfect. Weight shift, effortless. Follow-through, like Sam Snead's.

But nothing compared to the feel of the club moving through the ball. It was on the screws. The ball compressing against the club face felt smooth, like biting into a piece of See's caramel-filled candy. The ball jumped from the club. I knew it was a good shot. In midair, my eyes finally picked it up. Frozen clothesline on line with the pin. It hit the green and stopped twelve feet from the pin.

Suddenly, I knew. Make the golf team? I can do that!

P.S. I lipped the birdie putt and had to settle for a par.

P.S.S. I made the team.

Golf is an ageless sport. Recently, my cousin, Bob Modersohn, wrote to me about his weekly golf tournaments with his Over-the-Hill Gang.

We moved to Austin in 1986 and were offered a complimentary membership at the local private country club provided we exercised our option within ninety days of moving into our new home. Former governor of Texas, the late John Connally, had bought up about 100 memberships, which he gave to those families who moved into the community that he had originally developed.

Up to that time, I played golf about once a year at the annual tournament for those people who were working in 3M's International Operations. The first thing I did was to order a complete set of Ping irons, which were tops at that time. Eventually, I acquired a set of Taylormade woods. My handicap is over 30 and I don't see it getting any lower until I improve my short game. My drives are better than 90 percent straight down the middle and getting longer now that I am using Callaway "Big Bertha" woods.

My biggest problem is getting sufficient power into my drives to clear lakes, swamps, and canyons. This has been such a problem that my golfing buddies refer to one such obstacle on the eleventh hole as Modersohn's Gulch. My partial solution to my weak hitting has been to walk up to the front of the tee box to tee off, regardless of where the tee boxes are located on these four problem holes. Even then, my success in clearing the water or the rough areas is far from 100 percent. I do this even in our weekly tournaments with the Over-the-Hill Gang. It has been going on so long that no one yells at me anymore. They just chuckle and have come to know that they have to accept me on these terms if they want me to be a part of the Gang. Someday I hope to be able to tell you that moving to the front of the tee box is a thing of the past.

What is it that you want to do someday? Remember, someday implies the future. If you are serious about the things that you want to do, if you are serious about your goals and desires, don't put off getting started until that "someday" in the future. Get started now—today. Make a decision. Make a commitment. Make the commitment to yourself, because that's the kind of commitment that counts. If you break your commitment to yourself, you're the one who will suffer guilt pangs, not me or anyone else you may commit to. You, and only you, will be the one who will lose out in the long run.

When I make commitments to myself, I take them very seriously. It's kind of like making New Year's resolutions except that, to me, commitments are not to be broken as are so many New Year's resolutions. That's why I don't make resolutions, I make commitments. I'll give you a few small examples.

Hans is a runner, as you know. He is a dedicated runner, as you may have surmised. He is also a zealot when it comes to running, and he seems to think it's his mission to convert all nonrunners into runners. Naturally, because I'm handy, he often focuses on me. He tells me everything in my life would magically improve instantly if I would just take up running. "No, thank you," I tell him. "I do not, will not, run."

To appease him, I took up walking. To a runner, of course, that doesn't count. Nevertheless, I committed to walking, and I do so daily. I walk a minimum of forty-five minutes each and every day, rain or shine. Being a weight-bearing exercise, it's good for my bones, according to my doctor. It's also good for my heart and it helps to keep my weight stable. Fortunately, I live in California where I don't have to worry about snow, sleet, and ice. But I do have our three to four-month rainy season to contend with. When it rains, I walk, regardless. The only time I don't walk in the rain is if the current storm happens to include thunder and lightning. I really don't intend to be a martyr just to be able to say I walk daily, rain or shine.

Mostly, I walk with Charlie, my American Eskimo dog, known locally as "the little white dog" or "Charlie, the barker." He is both a little white dog and a barker. When we walk together, we walk briskly; after all, that's our joint purpose, to get exercise. We don't stroll or dawdle as some dog walkers do, stopping at every fire hydrant and telephone pole.

Often, I'll be shopping or running errands off my "walking" beaten track and someone will come up to me and ask, "Are you the lady with the little white dog?" When I admit, "Yes, I do have a white dog," the individual invariably replies that they watch me go by their home daily. "My, you walk a lot," is the usual comment. "You seem to be out walking every time I look out the window!" Occasionally, someone along my route will say, "I watch you go by every day. I think we could set our clocks by you!" As a rule, I've never set eyes on these folks before. Amaz-

ing to think that there are people regularly watching me from behind closed drapes and blinds while I never realize that I'm being observed!

Yes, I made a commitment to walking some years ago and, when I make a commitment to myself, I don't take it lightly. As I said, the only thing that can keep me from my daily walk is a thunder and lightning storm. Otherwise, I'm committed to it. If I don't, I feel guilty, and that's a lot worse than the hills that sometimes render me breathless or getting soaked to the skin when it rains.

My walking doesn't satisfy Hans, of course. He wanted me to go back to the gym and become the exercise enthusiast I used to be before I broke my leg and put my back out. "Hans! Do you know how time consuming that is? I'll never get any writing done if I have to change into exercise clothes, drive to the gym, put in an hour working out, shower, and change again. Give me a break!"

Instead, he gave me an in-house fitness trainer for a couple of sessions for my birthday two years ago. So now, in addition to my daily walk, I'm committed to a daily exercise session as set forth by my trainer. Except for two days off when I had a bad case of the flu last October, I haven't missed a day of exercise since I started my in-home routine.

Sometimes I enjoy my walking and exercise routine; sometimes I'd rather be doing something else. I do both because I made a commitment and because it's good for me in many ways. I'm healthier, I look and feel better, and I'm able to maintain my weight. My walking and exercise routines have become habits; therefore I find myself doing them daily without planning or thinking about it.

If a new health and exercise routine is on your future agenda, why not begin it now? Make the commitment to yourself and then do it for twenty-one days. I've heard many times that if you do anything for twenty-one days, it becomes a habit. From personal experience, I can say that I totally believe that.

Once it's a habit, you expect to do it, you look forward to doing it, and/or you feel guilty if you don't.

Yes, for whatever personally motivates them, runners run, walkers walk, exercisers exercise, and golfers golf. What is it that you want to do? Don't wait for a better day. The time is now. Do it!

Your "I Can Do" Review

In the area of physical fitness, what do you plan to do someday?

_____

_____

_____

_____

What is keeping you from getting started?

_____

_____

_____

_____

What are you going to do about that?

_____

_____

_____

_____

Ponder This

You can't build a reputation on what you're GOING to do.

—*Henry Ford*

12

What Do *You* Want to Do?

Zeroing in on Your *Goals and Desires*

> *Follow your desire as long as you live;*
> *do not lessen the time of following desire,*
> *for the wasting of time is an abomination to the spirit.*
>
> —*Ptahhotpe, 2350* B.C.

I've told you about a lot of people that I know who are doing their thing. Jewelry makers, writers, speakers, teachers, singers, dancers, runners, walkers, golfers, and others. Obviously, I could cite endless examples showing that, in addition to those already mentioned, painters paint, sculptors sculpt, quilters quilt, swimmers swim, skaters skate, skiers ski, sailors sail, salesmen sell, fishermen fish, flyers fly, weight lifters lift weights, and body builders build their bodies. I could go on and on; the list is virtually limitless. To sum it all up, *doers do!*

Perhaps your goals and desires fall into one of the above categories, perhaps not. It doesn't matter; people who are really sincere about doing what they want to do, do it! What *you* want to do—what you *really* want to do—is your desire and your desire alone. You must honor it, and *you must do it!*

The good news is that you are supposed to do what you want to do the most. Yes, you are supposed to do—you are meant to do—what you want to do the most! You came into this world with the inborn talent to do what you feel most passionate about; that's why it's a burning desire within you. If that's the case, and it absolutely is, isn't it about time that you honored that desire, talent, and passion and did something about it?

No one knows more about that than my friend, Allen Klein. I'll let him tell you about his inborn desire, talent, and passion, one that he discovered as a young boy:

> It all started out when I was about seven years old. My parents took me to see my first Broadway show, the original version of *Carousel*. I was mesmerized by the magic of the theater: the actors, the lights, the scenery, the costumes, the dancing, the music, the songs.
>
> I remember, too, that we arrived late for the show, so when it ended, I refused to leave. I wanted to see the part I missed. I thought that, like a movie, I could just wait a few minutes and it would start over again. My parents tried to get me to leave, but I refused. ''No, I don't want to go.'' I said. ''I want to stay and see the beginning. I want to see the part we missed. No, I'm not going, I'm not going!''
>
> My parents dragged me kicking and screaming out of the theater that day, but my heart never really left the theater. At that moment, I decided that when I grew up, I would be a scenic designer.
>
> At PS 64, the Bronx, New York, when other kids would do book reports, I would take wooden cigar boxes and create miniature stage sets. When other kids were asked what they wanted to be when they grew up, they would answer: baseball player, doctor, lawyer. I said scenic designer and then, of course, had to explain to the adults exactly what that was.
>
> During my high school years, when my friends would go play baseball every Saturday, I would

get on the subway and go downtown to see a Broadway show. I would sit in the second balcony—what I affectionately called "seventh heaven"—and for one dollar and fifty cents, I got to see such theater legends as Judy Holiday in *Bells are Ringing*, Mary Martin in *Peter Pan*, Liza Minnelli in *Flora the Red Menace*. How many of you saw *Flora the Red Menace*? No wonder, it only ran eighty-seven performances. But I saw it along with every other flop and every hit on Broadway. I even got to see Carol Channing in the opening night of *Hello Dolly*.

My high school summers were spent as an apprentice to the designer in summer stock. After high school, I attended Hunter College. During my college summers, again, I got a job in summer stock. But this time, I was no longer an apprentice, I was the scenic designer. I designed eight musicals and plays in ten weeks. Some of my musicals had as many as twenty scene changes and my budget was $75 a week. My salary was not much more than that.

Designing for summer stock was not easy. Sunday night immediately after the curtain came down, we would stay up all night to strike the set and put up the next one to get ready for Monday night's dress rehearsal. As soon as dress rehearsal was over, we would stay up all night again, fixing and finishing the set for the Tuesday night opening. On Wednesday, I would design the next show. And Thursday we would start building and painting it. This grueling schedule went on for ten weeks.

After college, I got into Yale Drama School, the most prestigious graduate theater school at the time. It was a three-year master's program. I got kicked out after the first year. I was told I had no talent.

"Wait a minute, wait a minute, wait a minute," I said to myself. "You can't tell me I'm not a scenic designer. I was a scenic designer every time I sat up there in 'seventh heaven.' " I was a scenic designer way back when I made pretty pictures in wooden cigar boxes. I was a scenic designer ever since my parents took me to see *Carousel.*"

Nevertheless, I was told by Donald Oenslager, head of the prestigious Yale School of Drama, that I had no talent, I would never be a scenic designer.

After I got kicked out of Yale, I got a job at Macy's in their display department. One day, we were setting up a window display with a huge cabinet. To have some fun, I climbed in, sat in a cross-legged Buddha-like position, and had my coworkers close the doors. Every now and then, when someone passed by, they would open the doors and I would bow slowly, rise back up, and they would close the doors again.

One time, they opened the doors, I bowed, and looked up to find my boss standing outside the window with his arms folded, silently shaking his head back and forth.

After this short-lived job at Macy's, I became an apprentice at CBS television and then, after passing a stringent union test, I became a full-fledged card-carrying member of the United Scenic Artists of America. While my fellow classmates at Yale were designing college productions, I was designing shows on national television.

At CBS, I designed the *Merv Griffin* and the *Jackie Gleason* shows for a short spell, and all of the children's shows. I became known as The King of Whimsy.

My biggest show, I'm sure some of you have heard of it, was *Captain Kangaroo*. How many remember watching *Captain K*?! What you saw was probably my set. I called the house that I designed for the captain Tinker Toy Victorian.

In addition to the captain's house, I also designed most of the props on the show. If Bunny Rabbit invented a machine that would trick Mr. Greenjeans into giving him some carrots, for example, I designed the machine. If Mr. Moose had a prop that tricked the captain into sitting in a certain spot so that Ping-Pong balls would drop on him, I designed that prop.

Then it hit me like a ton of Ping-Pong balls. Looking back at my journey to become a scenic designer, I realized I learned a very important lesson about achieving goals. I learned that if I was *passionate* about something, then *nobody, nobody, nobody* could tell me I couldn't do it.

Reread Allen's last sentence. Apply it to your situation. Know that if you are passionate about something, nobody, nobody, nobody can tell you that you can't do it. These days, Allen is passionate about two other things: professional speaking—his scenic designer story is an excerpt from one of his speeches—and writing books. With Allen's talent, desire and, especially, his passion, I don't need to tell you that Allen is extremely successful at everything he does.

I met Julie Church when a neighbor suggested I contact her because I was looking for an alternative to the kennel for Charlie and PK when I had to go out of town. It wasn't until after I talked to Julie that I realized that she was the author of one of my most cherished dog books, *Joy in a Woolly Coat: Living with, Loving & Letting Go of Treasured Animal Friends.*

I wondered how this University of Wisconsin graduate in elementary education, who had a minor in music, came to be running a grooming and boarding establishment for dogs out of her home. Julie explained that when she first came to California to teach in 1961, she was overwhelmed by the California scene. She left soon after, but the lure of California brought her back to "the scene" and teaching again ten years later in 1971. Things had not changed that much. Julie found herself increasingly dissatisfied with teaching, but could she actually stay home? Her husband was supportive, and Julie gladly gave up teaching.

At that time, our local newspaper, *The Montclarion*, was running a weekly column entitled, "Oh Grandma." The daughter of the column's author, Phyllis Bishop, who was a friend of Julie's, had a dog named Puppy. Knowing that Julie loved dogs, Phyllis asked Julie if she would care for Puppy on occasion for a nominal fee. "I can do that. In fact, I'd love to do that," replied dog-lover Julie. And that, as they say, was the start of something big! Julie started boarding dogs for friends and neighbors. One day, Julie opened *The Montclarion* to read in "Oh Grandma," "Puppy died today . . ." She was brokenhearted.

Julie's marriage started to fall apart. "What can I do to support myself?" she worried, not wanting to go back to teaching. Having provided home care and occasional taxi service to the grooming salon for a flight attendant's little dog, who required regular grooming appointments, Julie had become aware of a special need of many dogs. Haircuts!

"I can do that!" exclaimed Julie, as she thought of all the other scraggly haired dogs she'd been taking care of.

Julie believes in serendipity. That very day she opened the paper to find an ad looking for someone interested in training to be a dog groomer. That's how she added grooming to her repertoire of dog-care skills. Soon everyone in the neighborhood started taking their dogs to Julie for grooming and haircuts, saying, "Practice on my dog!"

But Julie wanted to take her service one step further. She had heard from elderly friends like Phyllis's mother that driving, in their later years, was becoming more and more difficult. "What if I could start a pick-up and delivery grooming-and-boarding service for my elderly clientele? And so this helpful and much appreciated service was added to Julie's repertoire.

Then one day in 1985, Julie was forced to write in her journal about her own beloved dog, Lady. "Lady died today . . ." How very reminiscent of her first association with other people's dogs when, so long ago, she read, "Puppy died today . . ."

Compelled to write about how much Lady meant to her and taught her through their only-too-brief years together, Julie embarked upon her book, not having the slightest idea of how to go about such a venture. Lady's death not only brought about this remarkable book, it took Julie on a spiritual journey that brought about a reorganization of her life. Julie said, "I thought I was the teacher, but I was wrong. Lady was not only my teacher, she created endless opportunities for my personal growth. She taught me patience and love, among so many other things. Lady is a symbol of everything I want to be."

An interesting serendipitous sidelight: When Lady died, a friend sent Julie a sympathy card with a picture of a group of animals on the front. Julie taped it above her keyboard and looked at it daily as she wrote. Some time later, when in Santa Barbara to attend a writing seminar, a participant suggested she look up Constance Coleman, saying, "I think she's someone you'd like to meet." When Julie arrived at Constance's cottage and was welcomed in for a cup of coffee, she saw a large painting on the kitchen wall. It was the original of the picture on the card Julie had taped above her keyboard. Yes, Constance was the artist who did that picture! And she went on to illustrate *Joy in a Woolly Coat*, of course. Julie says there is someone in the cosmos looking after and guiding her. I agree.

I think Julie's story is one of the most inspirational that I've heard. As animal lovers, we share much. But her story illustrates how it is possible to take something you love doing, in Julie's case, caring for animals, and make it into a money-making venture. Publishing a moving book about her relationship with her animal friends was a definite plus. The best part is that Julie absolutely loves her life and what she's doing. When I saw her surrounded by all her dogs—her personal babies and those she was caring for—I said to myself, "This is a truly happy woman!"

Cathy Le Blanc is a friend of Julie's, a neighbor of mine and, above all, a dog lover, as well. When she's able to take time away from her volunteer duties at the Oakland SPCA, Cathy practices her profession of interior decorating. But her love for animals and her passionate feelings for man's best friend continually encroach on the time she should be spending with clients.

But Cathy wouldn't have it any other way. In addition to the hours she donates to the SPCA, Cathy regularly receives calls at home—at least two a day, she tells me—from distraught animal owners requesting assistance in locating their errant pets, as well as from people requesting help in finding the dog of their dreams to adopt. And Cathy follows through on every call. "It's the least I can do," she told me. In answer to the inevitable question of how she can work with the increasingly large number of animals that will be euthanized if not adopted within a specified period, Cathy said, "I felt so very sad at first when I realized that some simply don't get adopted, and I still do. But I know that if I can spend some time with an animal, brushing or grooming him, or walking and playing with him, I'm adding to the quality of his life, regardless of how short it may be. Of course, my primary goal is to see that each and every one gets adopted. I do much of that on the phone out of my home."

Both Julie and Cathy are passionate about animals. Julie has forged her passion into a livelihood; Cathy's involvement is voluntary. They are both following their hearts and enriching their lives by doing so. Explore your passion. Perhaps you can turn it into a paying job; if not, consider becoming involved on a volunteer basis. Either way, your life will become far richer by your listening to your desires and following your passion.

I've been reading Bill Mann's radio and TV column in *The Montclarion*, the same paper that carried "Oh Grandma," for as long as I can remember. Before his affiliation with that neighborhood biweekly, Bill was a columnist for the *Oakland Tribune* for ten years. He's also TV columnist for the *San Francisco Examiner* and the *Santa Rosa Press Democrat*. In addition, he's TV critic for America Online.

Being a radio/TV person, I thought, "What a great job! You get to stay home all day and listen to the radio and watch TV. Then someone actually pays you to write about it!" So I called Bill to get his input on—in my opinion— one of the world's cushiest jobs. Bill told me, "The best thing about watching TV for a living is that you can spend twenty-four hours a day in your bathrobe."

"It's been a great life," continued Bill, who's plied his craft in such diverse cities as Montreal and Honolulu. When his first child, now college age, was born, he decided he wanted to be at home with his wife and child. He laughed.

"Imagine, being paid for staying at home with your wife and children!" Bill, who has a great sense of humor, went on about the pluses of being self-employed, "I always say, if you're going to work for a jerk, it might as well be yourself!

"I'm getting burned out, though," he confessed. "TV isn't what it used to be. But then, every subject area gets old. I'm looking toward changing fields and writing about the digital revolution and personal computers." Bill is passionate in his conversation as well as his writing. And he's the kind of guy who only does what he wants and likes. He'll do well—and enjoy himself to the hilt—regardless of his subject area, you can count on that!

What do *you* want to do? What do you *really* want to do? What do you want to do now that you're not doing yet? Have some of the personal stories I've related about people who *are* doing what they want to do helped to get your thinking processes going?

Perhaps you're like some of the people who attend my seminars about positive thinking. They're consumed with negativity. That's why they opt to attend. They usually hate either their jobs, their relationships, their mental and/or physical states, their surroundings, or all of the above. When I tell them they can change those things, often they will reply, "Maybe so, if I *really* knew what I wanted. If I knew what I wanted in the way of a job (relationship or other fill-in-the-blank problem that brought them to the seminar), I'd do something about it."

And they're serious. Not having a goal or clear-cut desires is not only a huge problem, often it is *the* problem. Having floundered around in that particular sea myself, I can relate. I call that time my searching period. What I was searching for was my purpose in life. I was relatively happy, I had no problems I could put my finger on, it was just that life had taken on a kind of ennui. Time was marching on and I wasn't accomplishing much of anything. Yes, I'd had an exciting, fulfilling life to that point, but I still felt an emptiness. There was something missing. I had always felt that I was put on this earth for a purpose, yet I was frittering away time by not doing something meaningful. It became my mission to find my individual purpose and act on it.

At about that time, I was asked to write an article for the NSA/NC newsletter. Those initials stand for National Speakers Association/Northern California Chapter. To challenge myself, I chose "Finding One's Purpose" as my subject. Obviously, the article was addressed to speakers, but I think the overall message can apply to everyone. Here is the article.

> As members of NSA, we might ask ourselves: "Why am I here?" and "What is my mission?" The answers to these all-consuming questions are to be found in our purpose. Everyone is here for a purpose and, rather than being a heavy concept, finding and following one's individual purpose is a liberating thing, because our purpose is invariably something we love to do, for which we have a talent, and at which we excel.

As speakers, rather than pursuing one's purpose, it is easy to become distracted by the desire to make money and to compete for status, acclaim, and the symbols of success in other areas. All too often we are encouraged to follow the trends, to get on the bandwagon of the newest hot subjects when our hearts and interests lie elsewhere. This is not to say we cannot approach new topics, but rather that we must discover and recognize our purpose and then adapt and incorporate it into our new presentations. When we are truly speaking from purpose, all of the good things of life will come to pass. Why? Because we are following the path to our destination.

How and where do we find our purpose? Look within. What turns you on? What, above all else, do you feel passionate about? What do you love to do? Where do your talents lie? Remember, you are never given a purpose without the talent to bring it about. If we're fortunate, we learn this early on; for others, it comes later. Introspection is the key. Explore the high points in your life—going back to childhood, if necessary. The clues are there! Remembering your uniqueness, your talents, and your passion and love for life will translate into your life's meaning—your purpose.

When you discover your purpose, you then have a responsibility—a responsibility to follow your purpose—into passion and then into presentation. With purpose, we can—and will—motivate, inspire, and encourage our audiences. With purpose, we, too, will become motivated, inspired, and encouraged. With purpose, we will become what we were meant to be. We will fulfill our destinies.

Now let's analyze what I said in the article and see how we can relate the message to you and your unique situation.

In the first paragraph I mentioned "mission." Mission has many meanings; one is "a task or function assigned or undertaken." In this case, your mission, or your assignment, is to discover your purpose and follow through on it. When you discover your purpose, you'll feel liberated because you'll see the path before you; you'll have a goal, a destination, something to strive for. To know that your purpose is something that you'll love doing is also liberating. How wonderful! And, to know that you'll not only find the talent within you to carry out your purpose, but that you'll also excel in doing it is also liberating.

In the second paragraph, I warn about following or searching for the symbols of success at the expense of your true calling. It's easy, sometimes, to get on the bandwagon just because everyone else is doing it, when your interests actually lie elsewhere. It's important to be true to yourself. Of course you can always adapt and incorporate current trends into your life while still maintaining a course aimed at your own unique interests. Remember, good things will inevitably come to pass because you will be following the path of your individual destination, the reason you were placed on this planet.

So, to the big question: How do you find your purpose? Look within. Spend time in introspection. Ask yourself what turns you on. What are you passionate about? What do you love to do? Where do your talents lie? Remember, and never forget, that you have an individual purpose and, because of that, you have been given the talents to discover and manifest that purpose. You are never given a purpose without the talent to bring it about. Explore the high points in your life, going back to childhood, if necessary. The clues are there. As I said in the article, remembering your uniqueness, your talents, your passion, and love for life will translate into your life's meaning—your purpose.

When you discover your purpose, of course, you then must assume responsibility; the responsibility to follow through on your purpose. With purpose, you will become what you were meant to be. You will fulfill your destiny.

Your "I Can Do" Review

The time has come to act on your goals and desires. List five that you intend to get started on now.

_____

_____

_____

_____

Pick one of the above and resolve to act on it immediately. List that goal or desire here.

_____

Think about your purpose. If you know what it is, or think you do, write it here.

_____

_____

If you are uncertain, list some areas in which you think your purpose may lie.

_____

_____

_____

_____

Ponder This

*Nothing contributes so much to
tranquilizing the mind
as a steady purpose—
a point on which the soul may fix
its intellectual eye.*

—*Mary Wollstonecraft Shelly*

13

~~~
⌖
~~~

You *Can* Do That!

Gaining Courage—Becoming Confident

> *You gain strength, courage and confidence by every experience*
> *in which you really stop to look fear in the face.*
> *You are able to say to yourself, "I lived through this horror.*
> *I can take the next thing that comes along."*
> *You must do the thing you think you cannot do.*
>
> —Eleanor Roosevelt

You've narrowed things down a bit. You've made a list—mentally, if not on paper—of the things you really want to do. Now you may be getting nervous, even fearful. *Can I really do these things?* you wonder, timidly. Of course you can! But make it easy on yourself. Take the items on your list one at a time. You can do that in two ways: You can prioritize and pick the most important item on your list, or you can pick the one that seems the easiest to you. I suggest the latter. Action builds confidence; once you've got one accomplishment under your belt, all of the rest are going to be so much easier.

Shirley Nice, a professional speaker and NSA colleague from San Francisco, told me about a recent accomplishment that I can definitely relate to: buying something that states "assembly required" on the box. Here is Shirley's confidence-building accomplishment story:

> What comes to mind when I think of "doing" is one of those obviously simple things—like

screwing in the legs of a newly purchased outdoor deck table. I have an immediate block when "assembly" is necessary and the little voice shouts, "Get someone else to do this!"—probably of the male gender. I had houseguests at the time, a young couple, and the husband volunteered to handle it. I was so delighted as his young wife extolled his ability to fix everything around the house!

After they left, I took a good look at my wooden deck table and I realized it didn't look like the one in the store. The legs were really at a strange angle and the outer rim of the table didn't fit together. I was about to call the store when I realized that it was assembled backward! There was no one to turn to; the item was too bulky and heavy to put in my car for a return. And as I stood there in helpless bewilderment, a new voice suddenly dared to faintly say, "*I* can do this!" And once I decided that, I did it! And it worked! It was the first time I had ever dared assemble an item from a store box, and I felt the pride of a craftsman! It's crazy, but I was really scared to face that old and well-established voice in my head. I still carry the voice, but now there is a new one, one that at least looks at the assembly instructions before calling for help.

Shirley's accomplishment was a relatively simple one when you consider accomplishments overall, but it's one of my favorite I-can-do-that stories because I so thoroughly relate to it. "Assembly required" absolutely turns on my fear mechanism. Next time I'm faced with a box full of parts, I'll remember Shirley and look at the instructions before crying out for help.

Now, take the first item on your list and, as Shirley did, let that new voice say to you, "*I* can do this." If the old, well-established doubting voice rears its head, drown it out by forcefully stating, "I *can* do this!" Then, following Shirley's example, once you've decided, *do it!* Feel the thrill of accomplishment, the pride of overcoming fear. Congratulate yourself. Reward yourself. Give yourself a treat. You deserve it.

Here's another story of what may be a small "I did it" to some and, to others, something for which to pat themselves on the back. I have a couple of friends back in my home state of New Jersey who phone me via conference call occasionally so that the three of us can gab together as we did in the old days. Jan usually initiates the call and, when she and Sherry are on the line, my phone rings. Fred, Jan's husband always supervised the operation but, one day when he was out, Jan got up enough nerve to try it herself. When I answered the ring at my house, there was much jubilation on both of their lines. "I did it, I did it," shouted Jan with glee.

Any time I hear either of the phrases "I can do that" or "I did it," I mentally or verbally say, "Wow! Great! Another I-can-do-that story." And that's what I said to Jan and Sherry that day. "I'm going to put that in my book!" I exclaimed.

"Oh, no, Alice! Don't you dare. We'd die of humiliation and embarrassment!"

"Why? It's an accomplishment that made you feel good, isn't it?" I queried, wondering why their pride should not be recognized.

"But it's so insignificant," Jan said.

"And Fred would really be upset," Sherry interrupted. "You know how he is, if you're going to brag about something, it had better be important!"

Obviously, I changed their names in this telling; I do want to continue speaking to them—and to Fred, as well!

I strongly disagree with their vehement disparagement of their triumph over technology. So it was a minus on a scale of one to ten; so what? Big or small, we all need to acknowledge and reward ourselves for our accomplishments, and the more the better. If we don't get praise from others, and we seldom get enough, that's all the more reason why we need to praise ourselves. The idea is to get in the habit of "feeling fear and doing it anyway," as Susan Jeffers says in her helpful book that expresses that sentiment, *Feel the Fear and Do It Anyway.*

Talk about feeling fear! Kata, and Marianna Nunes, another NSA friend, each contacted me separately, but within the same week, to tell me of their experiences with overcoming fear and gaining confidence through a program of extreme physical challenge. Perhaps you remember EST, Werner Erhard's very popular program of the seventies. I explored, but never underwent EST training, although many of my friends did, to mixed reviews, mostly positive. It seems that one of the EST programs was called The Six-Day. Both Kata and Marianne undertook The Six-Day; both said it changed their lives.

Kata was in or close to her sixties at the time she signed up. She wanted to prove to herself that she could do it, and she also wanted to prove to others that age should not be a barrier to daring adventure. When she related the rigors of the Six-Day schedule, all I could think of was the tales I'd heard about Marine Corps boot camp. The day started with a run at dawn; Kata was the last one in, the first day. Throughout the week, she worked up to being fourth from last. "That was okay with me; I never expected to win, but I did prove to myself that I was a winner," she proudly recalled. "That was important to me. The worst part of the program was the rappelling, which scared me to death," she continued. I had never heard of rappelling, which shows that I have no intention of ever considering daring exploits that involve ropes and mountains. I understand rappelling is the descent of a cliff or mountain by means of a double rope passed under one thigh, across the body, and over the opposite shoulder. Sounds not only frightening, but downright uncomfortable!

But that wasn't all. Kata went on to tell of traversing, another rope trick in which one zipped down the mountain and across deep ravines via ropes. "It was all so scary. But I looked fear in the face and said, 'I can do this!' And I did. I think I proved to the others in the program that they should never discriminate against anyone, and especially a woman, just because of age."

Marianna's Six-Day adventure elicited the same emotions, although she was not concerned about age and some people's inappropriate feelings of discrimination toward those in a certain bracket. Marianna was excited and challenged by the thought of breaking through unknown physical barriers during her Six-Day experience. She said, "If I can do that, I can do anything!" The best part, to Marianna, was beating her running time each successive morning. "It gave me so much confidence, I landed my first sales job right after that." Then she repeated, because it was the primary lesson that she learned, "I knew if I could do that, I could do absolutely anything!"

You, too, can have this firm, knowing philosophy. Once you start doing, you'll have the confidence to tackle previously untried challenges. Say to yourself, as Marianna did, "If I can do that (one of the things on your list), I can do anything!" And know that *you can do it!*

But there's more to Marianna's story. She didn't stop

with that first sales job; that was just a jumping-off place. Although she had previously been a teacher for ten years, Marianna always knew she wanted to be in business for herself; she had a fantasy that she could work out of her bedroom and make a lot of money.

With her newborn confidence, and upon the urging of a spiritual counselor who said, "Marianna, you *can* do that!" she started a consulting practice out of her home that soon became very successful. Then she saw Annette Goodheart, a speaker who did programs on laughter. "I was truly inspired by Annette. I thought, if she can do that, so can I. Annette became sort of a model for me, and the next thing I knew, I was speaking on humor. While I tell people that Annette catapulted me into my speaking career, it actually took seven years to get where I am today." Where Marianna is today is in the enviable position of being one of the most sought-after humorous speakers on the professional circuit.

Do you have an idol, a model, someone who inspires you and in whose footsteps you'd like to follow? If you learn everything you can about the line of work or profession you aspire to, and you train seriously, work hard, and totally apply yourself, there isn't any reason why you can't succeed handsomely, as did Marianna. Desire, passion, energy, and hard work can do wonders to propel you toward your goal. The more desire, passion, energy, and hard work you invest, the faster you'll reach your goal, whatever it might be. And there's no time like the present to begin!

Danny had a goal. Sometimes it seemed insurmountable. His goal was sobriety. He began many times to try to attain this goal: to quit drinking and become totally sober. Some people try all their adult lives to quit, without success. But Danny was determined that he would succeed. "My determination was all well and good," he told me, "but it didn't help when I found myself with a drink in my hands."

He tried all the usual things: Alcoholics Anonymous, the twelve-step programs, clinics, and treatment centers. Some would work for a while, then boom! He'd fall off the wagon again. "The worst part," Danny remembered, "was that I was a rotten drunk. I was loud and belligerent; not a likable guy at all." I found this hard to believe because Danny is one of my favorite people; he's sweet, gentle, and considerate. I simply couldn't imagine him in the role of a nasty drunk.

His frequent lapses were hard on his partner and on his mom whom he adores, to say nothing of being hard on him. "There were two really bad years back in the early '80s, when I'd go into treatment, be okay for awhile, then fall down again. I knew I was hurting all the people I love. But most of all, I was really hurting, and hating, myself." Danny stopped speaking as he remembered that difficult time.

I knew he hadn't had a drink in twelve years, so I asked, "How did you finally do it, Danny?"

"I went within myself," he told me. "I started doing relaxation exercises. I forced myself to let go of the problem. It didn't happen immediately, but gradually I found an inner peace. Then it was easy. We all have this built-in ability to help ourselves. The most important thing I learned is that it was all totally up to me. I found out that I have the ability to do whatever I have to do. Not twelve-step programs, not clinics or treatment centers, just me. We all have that ability. When it comes down to what's important in your life, you have to say to yourself, 'I can do that' and know that you really *can* do it. You've got to have confidence in yourself. My addiction is definitely a thing of the past. I am no longer tempted by drugs or alcohol."

Danny's is an important story. And a very encouraging one, as well. Fighting and overcoming an addiction is one of the most difficult tasks anyone can possibly face; countless numbers do not succeed. But there is hope. Heed Danny's sound words of advice: "When it comes down to what's important in your life, you have to say to yourself, 'I can do that' and know that you really can do it. You've got to have confidence in yourself."

You've got to have confidence in yourself. Make that

your motto. Better still, listen carefully to the words of the song, "I Have Confidence" from _The Sound of Music_ and make it your theme song. Sing along with Julie Andrews as the character she plays wonders what her future will be and worries why she's so scared to do things she's never dared. The song goes on to seek the courage that appears to be lacking and, finally, it concludes with "I have confidence in confidence alone. Besides which, you see, I have confidence in me!" Say those words over and over like an affirmation: "I have confidence in me!" Then believe it, because it is true. If you have confidence in yourself, nothing can stop you, absolutely nothing!

Jay Mulkey has renewed confidence in himself. I told you Jay's story in chapter 7. You will recall that Jay suffered from panic and anxiety attacks, agoraphobia, severe depression, and insomnia. His faith and his church helped him through this difficult period in his life. Jay called me last night with an addendum to his story. He had developed a bad case of bronchitis and went to his doctor; a chest X ray was ordered. When it was developed, the doctor called Jay back into his office. As he entered the office, Jay immediately felt an uncomfortable difference. The usually jovial staff was somber, as was the doctor. The X ray was on the screen and the doctor pointed out two major causes for concern: a greatly enlarged heart plus several lung lesions. "This looks very serious," he was told.

Jay told me that if this had happened the previous year when he was suffering from his many phobias, it would have sent him over the edge. "Now," he said, "I felt a tremendous calm. I had confidence that all was well; that a terrible mistake had been made regarding the X ray." Another picture was taken, and Jay sat in the doctor's office for what seemed like an interminable time, awaiting the results. "I was totally calm. No more racing heart, jangled nerves, and uncontrollable fear. I just had a total sense of confidence in my strong body and now-healthy mind. Regardless of the outcome, I knew I could handle it. I did think about all the things I still want to do in life, but I

guess anyone would go through that thought process under the circumstances.''

The second X ray was totally normal. What was the problem? What could have caused such a frightening diagnosis? Evidently, the technician had inserted the film into the machine improperly, or had caused it to move while the imprint was being made. Whatever, all is well. ''Once you face something like this, there's not much more to be afraid of,'' Jay related. Then he laughed and said, ''How else can they scare you at the ripe old age of thirty-eight!'' He summed it up with, ''I looked fear in the face and felt confident and in control of all my old anxieties. I still have friends who suffer as I used to. I tell them 'If I can do it, if I can overcome, you can, too.' ''

''If I can do it, you can, too,'' is something I also find myself saying frequently to others these days. Mostly it's about writing, because people know, or soon find out in the course of conversation, that I'm in the midst of working on this book. ''Oh, I wish I could write a book! I've always wanted to—'' is the comment I hear most often. Sometimes I paraphrase the lyrics from an old song, ''Anything I can do, you can do better. You can do anything better than me. Yes you can. Yes you can. Yes you can!'' Look fear in the face, screw up your courage, have confidence in yourself, and do it—whatever it is. Remember, I have confidence in you!

Your "I Can Do" Review

Review your written or mental list of the five most important things you've decided you really want to do. List them here in the order you intend to approach them.

_____

_____

_____

_____

Write down any and all excuses you've used to avoid starting on your list.

_____

_____

_____

_____

Now, go back to the list of five above and place a definite start date after each.

Ponder This

*Courage is doing what you're
afraid to do.
There can be no courage unless
you're scared.*

—Eddie Rickenbacker

14

What Have You Got to Lose?

Exploring Pros and Cons

> *Losers visualize the penalties of failure.*
> *Winners visualize the rewards of success.*
>
> —Dr. Rob Gilbert

How many times in your life have you asked yourself, "What have I got to lose?" A countless number, no doubt. Whenever we take on a new venture or make a decision—major or otherwise—we ask ourselves that perennial question. We want to know the pros and cons. We want to know what it's going to cost us in both dollars and time, and sometimes there are other considerations, as well. Is it risky or dangerous, hazardous to our health? Are we liable to lose money, friends, or face? Will it enhance our image and reputation or possibly injure both? Will it make us happy, or could it boomerang and produce unknown repercussions?

Yes, we always have to weigh the pros and cons whenever we contemplate anything new. In making decisions, sometimes the choice is obvious; we know the answer in our gut. Gut reaction is often the best, most infallible decider; we simply *know*—without need to analyze—which way to go. I've made many major decisions that way and usually have had no regrets. In fact, I prefer that method of deciding; to me, it's so much easier than endless ago-

nizing over what to do, and then going through the inevitable doubt trip, wondering if I goofed, blew it, and should have gone the other way.

When I reflect back over my life, I can pinpoint exactly the good and bad decisions I've made. Perhaps I should say "inappropriate" decisions because they were inappropriate for me but not necessarily inappropriate for someone else. I'm thinking now of career decisions; personal mistakes tended to work themselves out. In my life, career moves were, for the most part, cast in concrete.

My first broadcast job was in Plattsburgh, a quiet, pleasant little city located on Lake Champlain in Upstate New York, sixty miles south of Montreal. I told you a bit about my crazy debut into broadcasting in chapter 1. Plattsburgh was fun, my broadcast jobs there—at both radio stations and the local TV station—were a blast. After five years, however, I felt I'd saturated the market, and it was time to move on. And it was. I had absolutely no regrets about doing so although making, what to me was a tremendous transition to an unknown Midwestern state with two children in school, was an enormous challenge. I only considered the pros; if the cons raised their inquisitive heads, I ignored them. There was no contest, and I've never had any regrets about that move.

I was equally happy, perhaps even more so, at KSOO-TV in Sioux Falls, the Midwestern state mentioned above. But then, when romance entered my life, and later, when it seemed to go sour, I determined to remove myself from the problem—or rather, the man. So I auditioned and was accepted at a larger, more prestigious station in Wichita, Kansas. Bad move. Bad vibes. Bad gut reaction. But I didn't listen to my quiet advisers; I went ahead and tore up stakes and moved anyway. I wanted to get away. It was a disaster in many ways. There was nothing wrong with the new station or with my new and better job assignment; the problem was with me. The time wasn't right—or perhaps I hadn't come to grips with my emotional attachment.

Fortunately, I was able to reverse things. Three months

later, I was accepted back at the Sioux Falls station with a new and more stimulating assignment. Best of all, especially for my son, the house I had been renting had not yet been leased to anyone else, and I was able to move back into the same home in the same neighborhood. Mark was reunited with his old friends and went back to his old school. That experience taught me a lot about gut reaction. I now respect that deep, inner feeling, and I usually try to let it guide me.

Inevitably, the Sioux Falls odyssey came to an end as well. That happened after I made a visit to California to visit my daughter, who transferred from Syracuse University to enroll in San Francisco State. California was gorgeous, beautiful, warm, and wonderful—everything I could hardly believe existed on this planet. After living in such "garden spots" as Nome, Alaska, Limestone, Maine, Plattsburgh, New York, and Sioux Falls, South Dakota, I honestly didn't realize that there were places that did not have snow above the waist and temperatures below freezing much of the year. In addition, California had seashores and mountains, trees and flowers, and moderate temperatures year round. To me, it was paradise. I instantly resigned my KSOO-TV job upon my return from my California vacation and, without a qualm whatsoever or even a job offer, I set off for the Golden State. Good gut reaction. Good decision. No regrets.

All of this is to tell you to honor your gut reaction when deciding upon something new and different. If it doesn't feel good, forget it. If you have to talk yourself into it, forget it. If, on the other hand, it seems to fit and feels comfortable, like slipping your hand into an elegant kid glove, go for it. It's probably right for you.

Kata, who has one name like Cher and Madonna, and whom I mentioned earlier in regard to her Six-Day experience back in the '70s, recently told me about her "big decision and monumental adventure."

"The nerviest thing I ever did in my life was to go to Europe alone many years ago. My business was at its peak,

I had thirty-three employees, and was well regarded in the industry. I had a beautiful home and beautiful grown daughters. But I had a need to prove something to myself. I decided to move to Italy for a minimum of six months. I rented my home and put my capable managers in charge of my business. Why Italy? I'm not sure. Italy just sounded romantic and exciting. I didn't know a soul there nor did I know a word of Italian. I wanted to see if I could operate without props.''

When I asked Kata what she meant by ''operate without props,'' she explained.

I wanted to see if I could live by myself without my baggage, my props, the people I tended to lean on. I wanted to get in touch with myself; just me without my usual support system. I think what brought it on was one day when one of my daughters said, "Mom, can I make an appointment to talk with you?" And she was serious. I saw how involved I'd gotten in worldly, material things—the business, making a living, managing people—and how far I'd gotten away from what was really important to me. I needed to find myself.

I talked with my kids and my managers about my fantasy. They all said, "Go for it," so I did it. I moved to this little town in Italy where I didn't know a soul and couldn't speak a word of the language. Scary? You bet! You can't imagine how many times, when I went to bed at night, I promised myself that the next morning I'd buy an airline ticket back to the U.S. But I stuck it out. I've never had any regrets. I wouldn't change that experience for anything. I proved to myself that I can do anything I want or dare to do. It gave me a real feeling of power. I may be considered an older woman now, but I know I can always do—and succeed—at anything I put my mind to. Age has absolutely nothing to do with it. Pros and cons? No contest. It was "go for it" all the way! What did I have to lose? Six months of my life. But that wasn't a loss. Far from it, it was an investment—the best I ever made in my life.

Kata is an exciting, vibrant woman, in addition to being beautiful. She exudes confidence. To bring her story up to date, she came back to her business and picked up the reins once again. Later, she married a dashing gentleman she met while in Italy. That didn't last forever; he had trouble adapting to American culture, and Kata felt Italy was too long a commute from her family and business. But it did add spice to her life for a good ten years. Kata has many more adventures to look forward to, rest assured!

Look over your list of wants, wishes, and desires. Consider the pros and cons of each. Ask, "What have I got to lose?" Then make a decision. Pick the one that's the most important—or the easiest—and start the wheels turning.

Dick Fitzmaurice, my radio buddy, dealt with a different kind of "turning." His "wheel"—so to speak—was a turntable. Dick was one of the greatest, most amusing on-air personalities I've ever had the privilege to hear. I say "was" because Dick is now in charge of PR for one of California's most prestigious corporations. But when we get together, radio is our subject. Here's Dick's story of how his on-air no-holds-barred personality came into being:

> Microphone on. "David Gates and Bread. That was 'If,' " I told the invisible audience. "Back with more sounds of the coast after this for Economy Drug." Microphone off.
>
> It was the 2,147,765th time I had played Mr. Gates's opus—plus or minus a half a million. It was the 3,675th time I had read the Economy Drug commercial—plus or minus one.
>
> "A zillion commercials, three public service announcements, seven promotional announcements every single hour," I muttered to myself during the next recorded spot. "This must be the most boring radio station in the world to work for. What do they want from me?"
>
> It wasn't the way it was supposed to be. Ever since I got my first GE clock radio at age seven, I had wanted to be on the air. Here I was. Sure, it was only $625 per month, but I was doing what I wanted to do. At least I was until I started counting. Now I wondered if I could ever be the radio personality I wanted to be.
>
> Commercial break over—finally. Microphone on. "Two-forty-five on the Coast. ABC News at

the top of the hour. Here are the Bee Gees and 'Stayin' Alive.' '' Microphone off.

"I gotta figure my own way of 'Stayin' Alive,' '' I said out loud to the soundproofing. Then one of those little flashes of insight we all get—all too infrequently—hit me. I could make $650 a month sweeping floors at the local college. If I didn't try new things on the air, if I refused to take some risks, if I refused to grow, I might as well be sweeping floors.

"Let 'em fire me," I said to the Brothers Gibb as they revolved on the turntable. "I'm gonna have some fun here!"

Bee Gees over. Commercial break complete. Microphone on. "Let's play the San Luis Show-offs," I announced. "Give me a call if you want to show off your talent, listeners. You can sing, you can dance, you can play the piano or violin. Call me—you can do anything you want to do!"

The phones went wild. There *were* people out there! People ready to be entertained and people looking for a chance to display their own creative talents.

Two callers into the feature, a guy named Ron called to perform his talent for creating hand shadows of European countries. Bulgaria was his speciality. Italy was a no-no, banned by the FCC as an obscene gesture!

The boss popped his head in the studio. ''Great bit!'' he said.

Radio personality? You bet—I can do that!

And that was the beginning of Dick's many famous and funny radio bits. When we get together and he gets started reminiscing about some of his on-air escapades, I simply go into stitches. But the important message that Dick gives us in this story of his on-air personality's beginnings is this, and I'll repeat his exact words: ''If I didn't try new things on the air, if I refused to take some risks, if I refused to grow, I might as well be sweeping floors.''

Let Dick's sage words apply to your situation. If you don't try new things, if you refuse to take some risks, if you refuse to grow, you might as well be sweeping floors. Ah, the life of quiet desperation! Don't let it happen to you!

In a recent ''Dear Abby'' column, I was intrigued by the heading: ''It's Not Too Late to Change Your Life.'' A reader from Twin Falls, Idaho, wrote Abby to tell about important changes that took place in her life and her husband's. She said that when most of their friends were settling down to an empty nest, circumstances threw their lives into a state of flux: a major job move for the husband and a new career for her.

In discussing what she should do career-wise, her daughter asked what she would you do if she could do anything in the world she wanted to.

''Teach mathematics,'' was the prompt reply.

''Go for it, Mom,'' urged the daughter.

''But it's too late,'' worried the mother, stating she'd be fifty-two years old when she got back to the workforce. Then she remembered Abby's advice to another reader: ''Never put off starting something because of how old you'll be when you finish.''

So the woman enrolled in college and graduated with a bachelor of science degree—magna cum laude! She concluded her letter to Abby by saying, ''I like teaching more than I thought possible. My life is filled with new friends, new challenges and most important—joy. I am grateful to my family for their support, especially my daughter for encouraging me to go back to college—and to you, Abby, for pointing out that I would have been fifty-two this year whether I went back to school or not.''

The letter was signed, Nancy J. Robinson, Twin Falls, Idaho.

What is your dream? What are you doing about it? Heed the advice put forth in the above-mentioned newspaper column: It's never too late to change your life! You have the ability to change yours. Start today! Ask yourself, ''What have I got to lose?'' Consider the pros and cons, and if there are no serious reasons why you shouldn't follow your dream, go for it!

Your "I Can Do" Review

Choose the first dream you intend to follow. Ask, in regard to that dream, what you have to lose if you follow it. List your answers here.

_____

_____

_____

_____

Continuing with the first dream on your list, consider the pros and cons of following that dream. List them here.

Pros _____

_____

_____

Cons _____

_____

_____

Continue this exercise with each of the dreams on your list.

Ponder This

You've got to create a dream.
You've got to uphold the dream.
If you can't, go back to the factory
or go back to the desk.

—*Eric Burdon*

15

——— ∞ ———

What's Standing in Your Way?

Confronting Obstacles—Real and Imaginary

The Wright Brothers flew right through the smoke screen of impossibility.

—Charles F. Kettering

You know what your dream is; you've identified your ultimate goal. What's standing in your way? What's your "smoke screen of impossibility?" Bev Bender's smoke screen was fear—the fear of taking risks. Bev is now a professional speaker and humorist, but back in 1979 when she got divorced, life wasn't so sunny and things weren't so funny.

When I think about challenges, I always look back to the summer of '79. I tell myself, "If I got through that, I can get through anything." When my husband and I divorced in 1979, we were living in Santa Cruz, but that's a relatively small town. I didn't think there were very many opportunities for me there in my new role as breadwinner and single parent. I really wanted to move to San Francisco, but I didn't know anyone in The City. I had to find a place to live, I had to get a job, and I hadn't worked in twelve years. Mostly, I was scared about making the move by

myself; I went straight from my parents' home into marriage. When we'd moved in the past, my former husband had always found a place to live and handled all the packing and other arrangements.

Now it was totally up to me. My daughters Debbie and Jennifer were nine and twelve at the time and, on top of everything else, I had to worry about getting them into good schools. In Santa Cruz, the school where Debbie went was real pretty with grass all around; the one in San Francisco reminded me of *The Blackboard Jungle*—I guess it just needed a paint job—but it turned out to be okay. I found an alternative school for Jennifer and that worked out fine for her, too.

It was my desire to move to San Francisco and the desire to start anew that got me through the fear. Relocating was exciting on one hand, but on the other, I recall it as a terrible time. One thing that helped is that I finally got my college degree, which I'd wanted for so long. That made me very proud of myself; it helped get me through the trauma.

My degree was in sociology, so I thought going into sales would be a good place for me, as a woman, to start. It was tough. In interview after interview, I was discounted because of my twelve previous years as a housewife. And I was really naive. No one wanted to take me on. Thankfully, I was finally hired by Paul Revere Insurance; they believed in me. Selling insurance is difficult if you don't have any friends or contacts, but I proved myself by establishing a good sales record through the hardest method possible, cold-calling. It was an anxious time—and a hard time.

I joined Toastmasters, too. That helped me open up a lot. Overall, when I remember those years, I remember the fear. It was a real obstacle. You have to learn to stretch yourself. Now, when I'm faced with fear, when I worry about risks, I *know* that *I can do it*. I know I can do anything!

Today, Bev's advice to those stressed out about work, relationships, and life in general is, "Lighten up! Put more humor into your life. It's fun, free, and nonfattening!"

Good advice, Bev!

I am particularly glad that Bev shared her story with me because I think it's an extremely important one for those of us who may find ourselves in her situation: divorce or, as in my case, early widowhood. Bev and I went through many of the same life-changing and challenging situations: having to relocate and all the trauma that goes with moving and establishing one self in a new community, assuming the role of single parent and breadwinner, finding a job, and making countless major decisions when before they'd been made for us.

It can be a scary time, but with each new victory or accomplishment, regardless of how minor, we stretched ourselves and grew. When we came out the other end, and everything worked out fine, the realization that "I did it, therefore I can do anything" is empowering and well-deserved.

Another speaker friend, Joel Rutledge, could write volumes about victory, accomplishment, and overcoming obstacles. My first recollection of Joel was that of a shy, sensitive, intense young man. When he spoke to me, I always had the feeling that I had his total attention because he looked at me with great concentration. I also noticed that Joel spoke slowly and carefully, as if weighing his words. I liked him instantly and I was pleased when, as a reporter for our local National Speakers Association newsletter, I was asked to interview Joel for an upcoming article.

Before I placed the call for the interview, the individual who gave me the assignment mentioned something about Joel's having disabilities. "What disabilities?" I asked. I was told that, for most of his life—twenty-five years, in fact—Joel suffered from severe stuttering. I was astounded! Obviously, he had conquered his stuttering; perhaps that was why he tended to speak more slowly than some of us and seemed to choose his words carefully. His other disability turned out to be his vision; Joel is so visually impaired that he is classified as legally blind. I would never have known had I not been told.

Joel is a very open person, and I felt quite close to him after the interview. That's why, when writing about overcoming obstacles, I instantly thought of Joel. He agreed to a second interview for this book, and we talked for a good long time; Joel has many stories and anecdotes to tell about his struggle through his past difficulties, especially the stuttering. With Joel, I feel I must discard the word "disability" because, to me, Joel is as normal—or more so—than most people I know.

Joel told me some interesting things about stuttering. When he was about twelve years old and stuttered very badly, he was able to easily read Christmas stories in a group, but never alone. He remembers reading very loudly because it felt so good to be able to get the words out. When in high school, he told about carefully choosing words that might be easier to say than others. Once, the answer to a history class question was "Canada," an impossible word for him, but he was able to say, "Our neighbor to the north." He was glad that we only had one neighbor to the north!

"Around stuttering, there's a huge amount of shame about expressing yourself and feeling like a freak," Joel confided. "People don't know how to respond, consequently they become embarrassed and uncomfortable." Joel is active in stuttering groups and projects. He told me that the most difficult thing for a person who stutters to say is their own name or to introduce themselves. "It brings up a lot of anxiety. It's important to give a person as much time as needed. Sometimes it takes five or ten minutes just to get your name out." In speech-impaired groups, there's such a depth of connection that, as Joel put it, "It's as if you're coming back from a war. Other people can't appreciate or understand it unless they've been there. Being with other people who stutter is very healing and inspirational."

Joel does stand-up comedy and has appeared on *Access to Comedy* on CNN-TV. He also appeared in the documentary, *Able to Laugh*, a film about disabled comedians. He told me a marvelous story of how, some years ago, when he was a restaurant janitor in the Noe Valley section of San Francisco, he practiced his routine for a seminar program entitled "Self-Expression" while mopping floors and talking to the toilets. "I knew if I could get through the opening," Joel said, "I'd have it made. I got a standing ovation at the seminar. It was a wonderful beginning for me."

Something I did when I felt especially fearful," Joel related, "was to look at a picture of myself as a small boy. Somehow, that brought me through the fear." I thought that was a powerful tool, indeed, and plan to explore it myself.

My take on the method is that you and I, as adults, might consider looking at the eager face and into the trusting eyes of pictures of ourselves as children, and consider all the potential pictured therein to be explored in the years and lifetime to come. Then, regardless of our present age, we must realize that we cannot let that child down. We still have the power and ability to fulfill some, if not all, of that child's potential. Try it!

Joel had many more wise things to say. The most important, I think, was his realization that, after many years of shame and pain, fear and embarrassment over his stuttering and faulty vision, plus his traumas relating to being brought up in an alcoholic, dysfunctional family, he was simply Joel. And, as Joel, he was absolutely okay just the way he was and is; that he no longer had to try to be like everyone else. Joel felt greatly empowered by that enlightened insight.

This is a message we would all do well to learn. We are all okay just the way we are; it's fruitless to try to be anyone other than our real selves. It is said that imitation is the sincerest form of flattery, but if you continually imitate others rather than initiating, cultivating, and honoring your own talent and style, you'll never be more than a poor imitation, a fake, and a phony.

Joel has a bright future as a speaker and entertainer. In addition to his obvious talent, he has the compassion and insight gained by living through very difficult times and overcoming the kind of obstacles most of us will never have to consider.

Martin Krieg underwent a kind of near-death experience that we rarely hear about. I met Martin when we both spoke at a large conference. He called me later to tell me how much he enjoyed my book and sent me a copy of his, entitled *Awake Again: All the Way Back from Head Injury*. Martin was in an auto accident that rendered him unconscious and almost brain dead. He was in a deep coma for many months. In trying to understand what was going on in his mind during the coma period, I asked Martin if he

was aware, if he knew what was going on and, if so, what
he was thinking.

When you end up in a coma, in a death situation
like I was, you don't have language. You can't
communicate that way, everything is just one—
the oneness we seek in meditation. To speak is
actually limitation. Not speaking is the most ex-
panded experience one can experience. I had to
be convinced that I was paralyzed and wasn't
speaking! It took me weeks to realize I was even
in a hospital. Finally, after people came to visit
and I couldn't leave with them, I realized there
was something wrong with me. Trying to overcome became man's work. I started pushing. I
determined to learn to speak again in order to
impress certain people. When I finally realized
something was wrong, I wanted desperately to
walk so I could walk out the door with my
friends. Walking is a tremendous task if you
haven't done it for a number of months. You suddenly realize the importance of every single mus-
cle and ligament. Fortunately, I connected with
Don Chu, an Olympic trainer and strength coach
who changed me, in my thinking, from being a
sick person to an injured athlete. Every day was
like the Super Bowl; every motion such utterly
tremendous work. I pushed so hard my hair hurt
and my face contorted. My inspiration came from
the injured athletes all around me.
    The hardest part of my recovery was becoming
acclimated to normal social conditions. I turned
to self-improvement books for my salvation, but
first I had to learn how to read all over again.
Then I became a walking, talking, self-
improvement think tank, ad nauseam! My biggest
key to recovery was that of diet; I began a mac-
robiotic diet, which I maintain today. It has

helped sustain my moods and energy reserves with a consistency I haven't known since before the car wreck.

Martin Krieg is now a public speaker and a prominent voice for head injury victims. His efforts to promote fitness have made him a popular national figure and have earned him several impressive citations. Currently, he's focusing his attention on the creation of a national bicycle highway and is planning to make a third cross-country trip to help promote this concept. In addition to his therapists and all the others who helped with his recovery, Martin credits his crash course in self-improvement books and tapes for where he is today, both mentally and physically.

You, too, can take advantage of such a crash course. Avail yourself of the many worthy self-help books at your local public library or bookstore. I heartily endorse this easy, inexpensive method of self-improvement and education. I personally prefer to buy such books after they come out in paperback, rather than borrowing them from the library, because I find I constantly refer to them. I have a substantial self-help library and consider these books to be my personal friends.

Campbell's story—or rather, my story about Campbell— was not one of fear or worry about risks as was the case with Bev Bender, or fear, pain, shame, and embarrassment as was Joel Rutledge's story, nor was it one that involved extensive rehabilitation, as was the case with Martin Krieg. On the contrary, to everyone who knew him, Campbell seemed totally fear-free and non–accident prone. In fact, he seemed to get his kicks out of taking risks, tempting the fates, and overcoming challenges.

Campbell was my high school sweetheart, my husband, and the father of my children. We met and eloped during the war, which altered the lives of everyone in the world at that time. Campbell enlisted in the Air Force just prior to his eighteenth birthday, at which time he could have expected to be drafted into the Army if he hadn't previously enlisted. During the war years, we lived the life of a typical military family, moving every few months or so, depending upon his schooling and assignments. Although he had hoped to become a pilot, that quota was full and, instead, he became a bombardier-navigator, graduating with the rank of Second Lieutenant.

When the war was over, although he had applied for a permanent or regular commission, he was discharged. To our dismay, we found ourselves to be civilians; his dream of becoming an Air Force pilot seemed dashed. As civilians, there were many new things to face and choices to be made: primarily where to live and what line of work he would go into.

Being a first-things-first sort of person, Campbell decided to tackle the housing problem and then worry about a new career. He determined that he would find us a nice plot of land and build a suitable house on that land. Naturally, a dream of that sort requires money, and I don't recall that we even had a savings account. Campbell never allowed minor concerns like money, or anything else for that matter, to get in the way of what he wanted to accomplish.

He scouted around the countryside and decided upon the quaint town of Florham Park, which was not far from our New Jersey hometowns of Maplewood and Millburn. He located an elderly woman who was considering selling off a portion of her Florham Park property. With his charm and persuasive manner, it didn't take long for Campbell to convince her that we should be the new owners of the parcel of land in question. The next step was to come up with a bank loan or mortgage to pay for the property and finance the building of the house.

My father was an officer in a large New Jersey bank; obviously that was the place to start. When Dad heard Campbell's plan, he laughed in his face. "Are you crazy? Why, you're barely twenty-one years old! You have no job, no line of credit, and no collateral. No bank that I know of would take the time to talk to you, much less agree to a loan! And then you say *you're* going to build the house?

What do you know about building houses? Have you ever built one before? Why don't you go about things in the normal way. Get a job. Build up a bank account. Then, in a few years, when you're established, maybe we can talk again."

I listened and absorbed the negativity, the kind I'd heard all my life, whenever I came up with something that I wanted to do. Campbell was undaunted. He knew someone, somewhere would support his dream, so he made the rounds of banks and other financial institutions, telling anyone who would listen of his plan. He eventually found a willing ear and a loan was granted.

One evening shortly thereafter, we were having dinner at Campbell's sister's home with his entire family in attendance. Campbell was going over some blueprints that he had drawn up for our dream house. Then I opened my mouth and I heard my father speak: "Who are you to try to build a house? Have you ever built one before? Of course not! Maybe a dog house, that's all. Do you even know what you're doing with those blueprints? Yes, you got a loan, but maybe you'll blow the money because you don't know what you're doing!"

I was relentless. On and on I droned with my inborn, programmed negativity. Campbell's parents, sister, brother-in-law, and Uncle Charles all looked at me in astonishment. I could read their minds: *How did she ever get into this family?* I was firmly told by one and all that if Campbell said he could do it, he could do it, And that was that! To this day, I remember with deep chagrin my embarrassment that evening.

Did he do it? Of course he did! The loan he was granted was for a minimum amount. He had to improvise. For one thing, he bid on and won an assortment of old military buildings that were to be torn down. The lumber in those buildings was seasoned and preferable to new lumber that he might purchase. But he had to tear down the buildings and hire a truck and helpers to haul the lumber to Florham Park. That was all accomplished with the ease with which

he did everything he tackled. Next it was digging a foundation, putting in footings, erecting the framing, and all the rest of it. Forgive me if I don't know the appropriate terms. Although I was on location daily with three-year-old Beverly, my assignment was clearing brush. As a result, I came down with the world's greatest case of poison oak!

The modest home that we had first envisioned had turned into quite a lavish enterprise as time went on. When the final plans were implemented and construction was nearing completion, a telegram arrived. It was from the Air Force. Campbell's regular commission had been approved; if he chose to accept, he had to reply within a short time limit.

What to do? Here we had a beautiful, custom home almost ready to move into. If we replied in the affirmative, we didn't know what the future might hold. But there was still the hope of pilot school eventually, Campbell's ultimate dream.

What did we do? Campbell opted to accept the Air Force commission, so we sold the house on Brooklake Road and looked forward to our new and exciting assignment, an overseas one, we were promised. I had visions of Europe: England, Germany, France, or Italy, glamorous places where service friends had been stationed. Our assignment turned out to be Nome, Alaska, not too far from the Arctic Circle. Alaska was not yet a state at that time and was considered an overseas assignment. To compound matters, his orders said, "No dependants will accompany."

"Ignore that," said Campbell with his usual positivity. "Anyone can go to Alaska; it's a free and open territory." So Beverly and I flew to Alaska and set up housekeeping in an old gold miner's shack. Several assignments later, Campbell went on to pilot school, became a jet pilot and, as they say, the rest is history. Campbell always succeeded in whatever he attempted in life. He never let a few negatives get in his way, even when it was his wife dishing them out, as I did when he decided to buy property, get a loan, and build a house for us; or when the Air Force said we couldn't go to Alaska and live there with him when he was issued that "glamorous" overseas assignment. Whatever the obstacles, Campbell always found a way to overcome them.

That's why I didn't believe the Chaplain and Campbell's Commanding Officer that pre-Christmas evening when they came to our front door at Loring Air Force Base in Maine to tell me that Campbell had been killed in a military air crash. They told me that something had gone wrong with the plane, the propeller fell off—turned out to be metal fatigue—and that Campbell had radioed that he would have to bring his plane in for a crash landing.

Campbell determined that he could make it to a small private airfield in Millinocket, a field on which he had landed and taken off innumerable times with our private plane. He said to the copilot, who survived, "No sweat, I know this field like the palm of my hand."

When they told me that he had crashed at the end of the runway at Millinocket, I was incredulous. "I don't believe you," I lashed out at the Chaplain and the Major. "Campbell *did* know that field like the palm of his hand. If he said he could bring the plane in, he could bring the plane in. You're keeping something from me, and I demand to go to Millinocket.'' Naturally, I was in a state of shock and disbelief. They refused, saying no one would be allowed near the crash site, especially the distraught new widow.

The hell with you, I said to myself, remembering Campbell's reaction when we were told we couldn't go to live with him in Nome. *Millinocket is a civilian airfield; the Air Force has no jurisdiction over it.* So I called John, the owner of the small airfield where we stored our private plane, and asked him if he'd fly me to Millinocket so I could look over the scene personally. I felt I would never be able to rationalize or understand the accident if I didn't see it for myself.

John landed his plane next to the still-smoldering wreckage of Campbell's military aircraft. I got out and walked carefully through the wreckage debris, picking up buttons from his blouse—the military term for jacket—and his belt buckle. Then I looked around and understood why he had not been able to bring the plane in for a successful crash landing. There, at the very end of the runway, was a trailer park inhabited by civilian families. If Campbell had been able to continue his flight path down the runway and past the end of it, all would have been well. But, upon seeing the trailers looming up in front of him, he veered to the left at the very last moment to avoid the small trailer community, causing the plane to flip, explode, and burn. This, too, was verified by the copilot who was able to jump clear of the wreckage and run for his life before the explosion.

Why do I bring this up? Why do I allow myself to open old wounds and relive that tragic Christmas of 1956? For two reasons: First, to show that even a confident person like Campbell had to put up with obstacles—those imposed upon him by his in-laws and wife—and second, and most important to me, to illustrate that positivity can come out of negativity, which I consider the most serious obstacle of all. This reversal in my personal thinking—from being the chronic negative thinker I was brought up to be, to becoming a positive thinker under the tutelage of Campbell—was a major turning point in my life, thereby changing it forever for the better.

I was brought up by cautious, fearful and, I hate to say it, negative parents. I appreciate their serious concerns, their caring, and their admonitions; most parental anxieties are well-founded. Accepting challenges and taking risks were not in their accepted mode of thinking; being safe, staying within accepted perimeters, and not rocking the boat were their guidelines. And I can totally understand that; after surviving a depression and my near-fatal childhood illness, before hospital insurance and antibiotics, my parents had much to be concerned about. My life seemed to be cast in cement by my upbringing and their philosophy, and I accepted it.

Meeting Campbell at a very early age opened up an entirely new way of thinking to me, a new attitude toward life that I never knew existed. Obviously, as evidenced by my negative reaction to his acquisition of the land and the mortgage loan, I actively pursued negativity to the point of almost ruining our marriage, until I finally woke up and truly assessed the situation.

When I became a widow at the age of twenty-eight, had I not been imbued with Campbell's I-can-do-that philosophy, I would have been lost, totally devastated, and probably could not have effectively relocated, raised my children as a single parent and, eventually, found a well-paying, rewarding career. Even though, in a split-second decision, Campbell sacrificed his life to save those in the trailer community, he chose to do that. What he left me, in addition to two fabulous children, was an attitude I absorbed over our years of marriage—an attitude of positivity, of absolutely knowing that I, or you, can do anything we put our minds to. What a gift!

In writing this book, I am passing this gift along to you. Please accept it.

Your "I Can Do" Review

What is your smoke screen of impossibility? Write your thoughts about it here.

_____

_____

_____

_____

Are you going to let these things come between you and your dream?

_____

_____

If not, what are you going to do about it?

_____

_____

_____

_____

Ponder This

*A man does what he must—in spite
of personal consequences,
in spite of obstacles and dangers
and pressures—
and that is the basis of all human
morality.*

—John Fitzgerald Kennedy

16

Don't Do It If—

Evaluating Risks—Doing What's Right for You

> *The scars of others should teach us caution.*
>   —Saint Jerome

Radio and TV newscasts and newspapers nationwide have repeatedly told the story and explored the details of the fatal air crash of seven-year-old pilot Jessica Dubroff, her father Lloyd, and flight instructor Joe Reid. By the time you read this, the story will be long forgotten by most, but it offers much food for thought for those pursuing a dream, as were Jessica and her father. If you do remember the story at all, you will recall that little Jessica was trying to break previous records and become the youngest person to fly coast to coast.

People across the country struggled to understand why Jessica's parents would allow a small child to undertake such a feat. The story was a natural for talk-radio as indignant, frustrated citizens explored their emotions. Many became angry with the parents, the authorities who allowed the flight to take place, and the media that exploited it. It was deemed a publicity stunt by some; others felt her parents pushed Jessica unnecessarily into something that was clearly beyond her abilities for their own aggrandizement, despite her naive but sincere desire to do it.

Jessica's mother defended the decision. In an interview with NBC's *Today*, Lisa Blair Hathaway said she did not consider telling her daughter not to fly across the country. "I did everything so that this child could have freedom and choice and what America stands for. Liberty comes from just living your life. I couldn't bear to have my children in any other position." Hathaway continued heatedly, "I know people say I make choices based on my children's well-being, not their safety. If it was about safety, they would be padded up and they wouldn't go anywhere, they wouldn't even ride a bicycle. My God, they wouldn't do anything."

Although not in total agreement, I marveled at Jessica's parents' recognition rather than their suppression of her inborn talents, desires, and ambition. In many ways, I admired them for their wholehearted encouragement of her desire to accomplish this feat, rather than forcing her into the state of anonymity and negativity that I had been placed in as a child, thus leaving my youthful dreams and ambitions unfulfilled.

Coming from our air-oriented family, I understood Jessica's I-can-do-that enthusiasm about the unprecedented undertaking. I doubt that I would have encouraged or permitted either of my children to do such a thing, but I was behind Jessica all the way. Not only was my husband a pilot, my son is a pilot, also. I clearly remember the day Mark took his first solo flight on his sixteenth birthday, accompanied by his very nervous but proud mother. Being sixteen is a far cry from being only seven years old. Nevertheless, I watched this adorable, precocious child with fascination as she went through her flight checks and talked with ease to the media. *This is a* real *I-can-do-that story,* I thought with admiration.

While she was supposedly at the controls, I was certain her instructor, Joe Reid, would be able to take over at any moment via the plane's dual controls should there be an emergency; therefore, I felt confident that all would go well and we'd soon have a new, albeit temporary, little heroine in our midst. A book or two plus a movie deal were sure to follow, thereby changing the lives of Jessica and her parents forever.

Sadly, their lives were changed forever, but not in the way anticipated. I don't think for a moment any of the three occupants of the plane or Jessica's mother truly considered the possibility of a fatal crash, or I don't believe they would have ever contemplated undertaking the flight.

But *why* did they take a chance on an overloaded plane? *Why* didn't they heed the dire weather forecasts and warnings? It was raining with icy conditions, there were severe winds, and a thunder and lightning storm had developed minutes before takeoff. Didn't they realize the conditions for takeoff at Cheyenne, due to the altitude and especially considering the weather conditions, were more difficult than in the California atmosphere where Jessica trained?

So what happened? What happened to the obvious cautions that should have been considered that Thursday morning in Cheyenne? To me, it appears that keeping on schedule was paramount; there were eager crowds waiting for Jessica at her next destination. The flyers didn't want to be held over in Cheyenne for what might have been days due to weather. Whatever the motivating reasons to go, two thinking adults put themselves and a trusting Jessica on the line and proceeded against all caution and reason.

My purpose in bringing up this tragic story is to emphasize caution in following your dreams. It is one thing to take risks, and we're urged to do so daily. It's totally another thing to deliberately ignore the obvious and to put lives on the line in the process.

Even small, seemingly unimportant acts can have dire consequences, as I well know. Years ago, when working in TV and living in Sioux Falls, South Dakota, I auditioned and was accepted for a supposedly better position at a TV station in Wichita, Kansas. The night before I was to depart for Kansas, I was horsing around the yard with my son Mark and some of his young friends. They had erected a high jump arrangement with a bamboo pole and were pre-

tending to be Olympic contenders. Although not very athletic in my youth, the high jump was something I had performed adequately, so I set about to instruct the group of boys on proper jumping procedures. They were enthralled that a mother could actually high jump, and I was probably showing off.

The problem was that I wasn't wearing appropriate shoes; in fact, I was wearing backless, heeled, wedge slipons that I liked because I thought it made my legs look good. Ah, vanity! Naturally there was no foot support whatsoever, and wearing even a slightly heeled shoe for jumping was downright stupid. In my defense, I must say that my becoming involved was totally spontaneous. I joined in on the spur of the moment and it didn't even occur to me to change shoes. My first few jumps went well but, as the pole was raised and the feat became harder, I fell, of course. And, of course, I broke something vital, a major bone in my foot. I ended up in a cast for a couple of months, thereby greatly hindering the transition to my new job and my upcoming on-camera duties. It was my fault because I did not think ahead and take proper precautions such as changing into appropriate shoes.

The upshot was that my new, exciting career took off,

literally, on the wrong foot. I was uncomfortable, awkward, and miserable. Everything I had to do was time-consuming and difficult: moving and settling into a new house, getting around the station and the set on crutches, driving, shopping. As a result, at the end of the day, I was exhausted and had no time for new friends or a social life. The entire time was a nightmare, and I had no one to blame but myself. In a very down mood, I decided the new job wasn't for me, so I resigned and, fortunately, was accepted back at my old station in Sioux Falls.

Don't let something like that happen to you. It only makes sense to exert caution in everything you do. Don't lose out on your dream when common sense and advance thinking can usually alleviate any potential problems.

My friend Hans, as you know by now, is a marathon runner. As I write, he is running the one hundredth Boston Marathon along with approximately 40,000 other runners. This year's large number of participants was due to the century celebration of the nation's first and most prestigious marathon.

To fill you in on the background, a marathon is a long-distance endurance race named for Marathon, Greece, from which, in 490 B.C., the runner Pheidippides carried news to Athens of a Greek victory over the Persians. Legend has it that Pheidippides dropped dead after arriving at his destination in Athens. And no wonder! Running 26 miles, 385 yards, or 26.2 miles, is not for the faint-hearted or the untrained. Pheidippides undoubtedly had not trained in advance to run that distance. But Hans, and all the other serious runners participating in the Boston event, as well as all other marathons, know they must train for months in advance in order to be physically ready for such a grueling ordeal, one that the human body is not made for.

In addition, Hans takes very good care of his health and body, and he has complete physicals annually. One of Hans's major dreams was to run the Boston 100; he knew the risks involved, and he took precautions in the way of training and regular physicals to assure that his dream would have a happy ending. He also knows that after the race, his immune system will be down; consequently, before and after every race, he increases his intake of vitamin C and other essential vitamins. Many marathoners come down with colds on their flights home due to the recycled, germ-laden air in commercial airliners. All of this only makes good sense, and I urge you to do the same if you are or plan to become involved in a high-intensity, endurance activity.

Sometimes, after pursuing a dreamed-of goal for years, you realize it's either not right or is no longer right for you. That's the story of Michael Lee of Seminars Unlimited, and here is the letter he sent me telling me about his experience:

> Have you ever set a goal, reached it, and then found that others kept pushing it out of your reach? Well, this happened to me in my quest to become a movie actor. Acting is something I discovered I enjoy doing more than anything else in the world.
>
> In 1977, I decided that I wanted to be a movie actor. This is not an unusual goal for a twenty-seven-year-old man who had been involved in the media since 1972 as a television producer for the ABC Television network. With this background, I was not just a starry-eyed dreamer, I was a realist with a plan.
>
> My plan led me to attend the American Conservatory Theater training program and move to Los Angeles to study at the Lee Strassberg Theater Institute in Hollywood. During the late 1970s, I starred in some of the most popular stage plays on the West Coast including *Year of the Dragon*. Using these credentials, I obtained a talent agent and was cast in some substantial roles in television and in films.

I was featured with Robby Benson in *Die Laughing* as a drummer in his rock 'n roll band and as a chauffeur with Chevy Chase and Goldie Hawn in *Foul Play*. Then my budding acting career seemed to hit a roadblock.

I began to realize that there were very few movie roles for Asian American actors. Think about it; name one living Asian American actor. Most people can only think of Bruce Lee, and he has been dead for over twenty years!

It became clear that after all of my years of painstaking acting training, the only roles that would be available to me were those of karate instructor or gang member. There's very little acting skill required to knock someone out with a karate punch or threaten him with a baseball bat!

Even today, racial and sexual stereotypes continue to persist in the media. It's not an accident that most Asians seen on television or in films are gangsters, Hispanics are portrayed as lazy or as drug dealers, African-Americans are usually featured in comedies, and women are housewives or weaklings.

After turning down stereotypical role after stereotypical role, it didn't look like I was going to get a chance to do any real acting, so I had to make a difficult decision. I could stay in Hollywood and do occasional bit parts, or I could take control over my life and leave Tinsel Town. So, I left, sold my home in the Hollywood Hills, and ended up teaching acting and television production for several years at colleges and universities. But this is only the beginning of the story, not the end.

As a result of my acting and teaching experiences, I have been asked by many companies to train their salespeople on how to use acting techniques to improve sales. In response to the demand, I developed a very popular course called "Developing Sales Charisma."

Ironically, one day while speaking to a group of 300 people, it dawned on me that I have already achieved my original goal of becoming an actor. I realized that professional speaking is the finest form of acting in the world.

Just imagine, if you don't develop rapport with your audience, they'll boo you off the stage. Speaking is even more demanding than acting since there are no retakes when speaking to a live audience. Speaking leaves no room for error, because there are no other actors who can help you if you forget a line. However, like acting, the applause at the end of a great speech or seminar signifies that you have given a great performance while impacting your audience's lives.

Today, I have never been happier. I have the privilege of traveling throughout the world and speaking to thousands of people each year. I've

found professional speaking to be just as rewarding as acting, and the work is certainly more
steady. I get to write my own scripts and *none* of
them has anything to do with karate.

The moral of the story is that we can achieve
our goals in many ways—sometimes when we
don't even realize it. Never give up, because the
mind is a powerful and magical device. When
you set it to work to achieve a goal, it *never* stops
working until *you* tell it to.

Right on, Michael! Let me repeat his powerful closing
statement: "When you set your mind to work to achieve a
goal, it *never* stops working until *you* tell it to." Put your
mind to work on your goal *now*. And while you're at it,
check to see if there are any obvious cautions that you
should observe in order to insure that all goes well and as
planned. After you've done that, *get started*. Don't let anything stand in your way!

Your "I Can Do" Review

In considering the dreams you've decided to follow, list the precautions, if
any, that you should undertake before
starting on your new venture.

_____

_____

_____

_____

Is your dream right for you, or does it need to be modified somewhat? Write your thoughts here.

_____

_____

_____

_____

Ponder This:

There are risks and costs to a program of action, but they are far less than the long-range risks and costs of comfortable inaction.
—*John Fitzgerald Kennedy*

17

Doing Whatever It Takes

Perseverance and Determination

Victory belongs to the most persevering.

—*Napoleon*

Here is quite possibly the most important sentence in this book: If you do whatever it takes, you will achieve your goal. Let me repeat that: *"If you do whatever it takes, you will achieve your goal.*

Does that sound overly simple? Too easy? Let's analyze the opening phrase. *If you do whatever it takes . . .* Just what does that mean? It means exactly what it says. It means that, when pursuing your goal, *you must do whatever it takes,* pure and simple. There is no other way.

As previously discussed, if you want to be a writer, you must write. You must address yourself to the blank page and put words on it. The words do not get there by osmosis; they get there because you put them there. That's what it takes to become a writer. If you want to be a speaker, you must open your mouth and speak, preferably in front of a group of listeners, and deliver a message about something that turns you on. That's what it takes to become a speaker. If you want to be a singer, dancer, skier, skater, or (fill in the blank), you must sing, dance, ski, skate, or (fill in the blank.) You do not, can not, will not achieve your goal by wishful thinking, daydreaming about it, or even by buying it. The way you achieve your goal is by *doing* it, period.

The remainder of the sentence: . . . *you will achieve your goal,* follows as night follows day. The complete sentence is a prime example of cause and effect. If you do whatever it takes, you are instituting the cause. The effect is that you will achieve your goal. This is an irrefutable, basic law of the universe and our existence.

When the full impact of cause and effect finally sinks into your mind, you will get an ah-ha! experience because it is so profound. This knowledge is the most powerful, liberating message you can ever absorb. Knowing that you have the power to institute cause in your life, thereby dictating the effect you desire, gives you total responsibility over your existence and future.

Now the arguments start flowing in: "I did everything to lose weight, but I stayed the same or gained." "I tried my best to stop smoking, but I still do!" "I wrote a book but no one will publish it." "I work my fingers to the bone, yet I can't seem to save a penny."

Valid arguments. No one ever said it would be easy. But I said, "If you do whatever it takes, you will achieve your goal." Sometimes it may appear that the goal cannot be achieved for some reason. In the case of the weight problem, perhaps there is an underlying physical reason why you seem unable to lose weight. Are you doing so under a doctor's supervision? Obviously, if you did not put excess food into your mouth, chew and swallow it, and if you indulged in appropriate, regular exercise, you would not gain weight, you would lose weight. However, if you have a thyroid problem or some other physical or hormonal imbalance, you should not fool around with diets and prescribing a weight loss program on your own; you must follow your physician's directions implicitly. However, if under proper supervision, you do whatever it takes, you will lose weight!

In the case of the smoker who cannot seem to quit, the question is, "Who puts the cigarette in your mouth and

who lights it?'' If you do one or both, you have no one to blame but yourself. You are not doing ''Whatever it takes'' which is *not* putting the cigarette into your mouth and lighting it. New research proves that nicotine is severely addictive, to the same degree as heroin or cocaine; therefore smoking is an extremely difficult habit to kick. But countless people have done so. They did whatever it took and they achieved their goal of being smoke-free. You can, too, if you do whatever it takes, that is, if you do not permit a cigarette to enter you mouth again, ever.

You say ''I wrote a book, but no one will publish it.'' That has happened to many authors. They then had to choose: to give up and let the manuscript gather dust on the shelf or to persevere, continuing to send it out to additional prospective publishers, or, they, and you, too, could

self-publish. Many self-published authors have creatively marketed themselves and their book, and later had their book bought by a large publishing house, then finally saw that book become a best-seller. It can be done if you do whatever it takes! I understand Wayne Dyer's first book, *Your Erroneous Zones* was self-published. Dyer filled his station wagon with his self-published edition and toured the country creatively marketing himself and the book. The rest is history, of course. Wayne Dyer is one of America's best-loved and most prolific authors and speakers, with many best-selling books, audiotapes, and videotapes to his credit.

Another excuse I often hear is the one voiced earlier: "I work my fingers to the bone, yet I can't seem to save a penny." This is a universal problem and one of the most difficult to address. Nevertheless, countless people nation-wide do manage to build up savings accounts, sometimes substantial ones. How do they do it? They do whatever it takes! You can, too! Recently I read of a seemingly poor, uneducated woman who never went past the second grade in school. She took in ironing all of her life. She managed to put her children through college and, if that wasn't enough, she gave an endowment to a black women's college so that "other women will become educated and won't have to work as hard as I've had to all my life." I think that's extraordinary! She didn't go on welfare, she didn't gripe and complain about her situation and circumstances. She did whatever it took to achieve her goal, she worked her fingers to the bone, almost literally, by ironing for other people all her life in order to educate her children and others she'll never know, so they can live easier lives than she did.

Yes, you must do whatever it takes, you must persevere if you would achieve your goal or goals. Webster defines persevere as "to persist in a state, enterprise or undertaking in spite of counter influences, opposition or discouragement." You must, as Winston Churchill said, "Never give up. Never. Never. Never."

That was my motto when I got into airtime sales at KPAT Radio in the late sixties. For the most part, women were not into outside sales at that time. I was laughed at by John, the sales manager, when I stated my desire to become part of the sales staff. "It's a jungle out there on the street. You'll never survive," he warned me. But I had previously spoken to the station owner; I must have impressed him with my enthusiasm, desire, and willingness to do whatever it takes to fill a substantial quota. The owner encouraged John to transfer me from copy to sales for a limited probation period. After getting the word from the big boss, John had no choice but to do so. I was reluctantly allowed to join the all-male staff, thus making one and all nervous by my feminine presence. I was given a probation period of six weeks. If I didn't produce by then, it was back to the copy desk.

I had to deliver; that was all there was to it as far as I

was concerned. I had to do whatever it takes. John, who was a sports enthusiast, determined that the station would be the Boat and Yachtsmen's Station in the summer months and the Skier's Station in the winter months. Being summer, my assignment was to sign up businesses and services relating to all phases of the boating world. This was basically virgin territory; boaters did not advertise on the air; they put their advertising money into boating and yachting periodicals and other efforts visible to their prospective customers, the boaters, sailors, and yachtsmen. The other members of the KPAT sales team continued with their regular, established accounts: car dealerships, banks, large stores, shopping malls, businesses having seasonal sales, etc., while I set out to obtain clients in the world of boating.

What I knew about boats, yachts, and anything to do with the world of sailing could be put into the eye of a small needle. My total exposure to the world of water vehicles was my single outing on a rowboat at Girl Scout camp. I didn't feel like a credible representative for their industry, but I had to do whatever it takes. I felt I could devise successful sales strategies and develop winning advertising campaigns for anyone I might sign up, but how to get to them in order to sign them up? I'd heard about the horrors of cold-calling, and I doubted my talents in trying to make a pitch over the phone or by dropping in unexpectedly on potential clients.

The one thing I felt strongly about was my total belief in the power and effectiveness of radio advertising. I also believed completely in my ability to write appropriate, selling, ad copy for any clients; I'd been doing that for years. The challenge I faced was in getting an audience with the prospective client so that I could convince him or her about the effectiveness of radio. In the case of the boaters, radio was something brand-new, an untried medium.

After much thought, I came up with a plan. I got all the Yellow Pages directories from the San Francisco Bay Area and made a list of every single prospect associated with every phase of the boating business. They were all over the map, geographically. If I'd relied on cold-calling, I'd truly be spinning my wheels—and wasting a lot of gas, besides. I had to make sure I had appointments in advance, so that I wouldn't be wasting time and money—and my short probation period in the sales department.

I called each of the businesses on my list and found out the name of the owner, manager, or decision maker. Nearly all of them were male. Then I put my plan into action. The first week I sent out letter number one, which read simply:

> There is a woman in your life . . .

A few days later I sent out letter number two:

> There is a woman in your life . . .
> She's 5' 3"
> 115 lbs.
> and she has blond hair and green eyes . . .

The last letter stated:

> There is a woman in your life . . .
> She's 5' 3"
> 115 lbs.
> and she has blond hair and green eyes.
>
> Her name is Alice.
> Expect her call.
> She wants to talk to you about Sails . . .
> and Sales.

At the bottom, I attached my business card stating that I was an Account Executive for KPAT Radio.

Then I took my list and, starting at the top, I called each and every one to whom I'd sent the series of letters. All I had to say was, "Hello, this is Alice from KPAT . . ." and that's as far as I got. Invariably, the response would be, "Alice! I've been waiting for you to call. When can we get together?'' My appointment calendar became fully booked; cold-calling was totally unnecessary. I knew radio advertising inside and out and was able to point out its many benefits to my prospective clients and devise appropriate campaigns for them.

I soon learned much about the world of boating; I had many willing teachers! All in all, it was a hugely successful campaign. Needless to say, I never had to worry about my probation period expiring. I was immediately accepted as a respected air sales representative. Within two years, I became Sales Manager when John went on to become a sports commentator on another station. Two years after that, I became General Manager of the station. All because I consistently did whatever it took.

There's an interesting sidelight to my "There is a woman . . ." story. I got to know all the movers and shakers in the world of boating and was frequently invited to attend their many parties and various functions. Everyone remembered with amusement my "There is a woman . . ." campaign and I was often teased about it. At one party, I entered the deck area and one of the boaters called out, "Oh, there's the woman in my life!"

Another countered him, replying "You're wrong. She's the woman in *my* life!"

Everyone laughed; this had become a regular thing.

Then, across the room, I noticed a red-haired woman who was obviously very angry. She was arguing with her husband who, she believed, was fooling around with another woman. "So that's her!" she screamed. "I knew there was another woman in your life! Let me get my hands on her. I'll strangle her and throw her wretched body in the bay!"

She flew across the room at me and grabbed me by the throat. Needless to say, I had a lot of gallant gentlemen come to my aid! But the perils of being in sales . . .

I've told this "There is a woman . . ." story, along with some of my other unusual sales approaches, many times at sales conferences, usually to an amused response. At a recent talk to unemployed salespeople, I received some criticism; the feeling being that my story was not a businesslike example of appropriate sales tactics. Perhaps not; it did succeed handsomely, however. In addition, it propelled me into being the consistent number-one salesperson on the KPAT staff and, eventually, into holding that station's two most prestigious positions. Obviously, I am a strong advocate for doing whatever it takes!

My cousin Bob, also being a Modersohn, is as persistent as I; it must run in the family. He wrote me about a time, many years ago, when he attempted to learn to water-ski. "My friends in Minnesota owned a power boat that they used to pull their children on water skis around the local lake. All the kids used to pop up like corks the instant the boat took off. Eventually they convinced me to take a turn at it. Every time I attempted to get water-borne, I ended up getting a dunking. This happened over the course of weeks for at least ten unsuccessful tries. Finally on the eleventh attempt, I got up for my first ride. After that time, I never again took a dunking. It has pretty much been the same story all my life. Rarely have I succeeded on my first try. Success has always been the result of never giving up—and learning from my past mistakes."

Let us all heed Bob's valuable words: "Success has always been the result of never giving up—and learning from my past mistakes." Take Bob's advice and persist. Never, never give up. As he did, you can learn from every experience. Every so-called mistake can have a positive outcome. If Bob had given up after his tenth try, he would never have learned to water-ski. On his eleventh try, he made it and never fell again. Whatever your goal, don't give up prematurely; one more try may be the one that takes you over the top from failure—better known as a "learning experience"—to success.

Another cousin, H. Phelps Potter, Jr., M.D., whom we call Phil, had another kind of water story to tell.

Swimming has always been one of my favorite leisure activities, but once it nearly killed me. My mother couldn't swim at all and my father wasn't much better. Wisely, my parents understood the importance of learning to swim and saw that my sister and I had appropriate lessons at an early age. We received instructions at a municipal pool and at summer camps where swimming was a major activity.

Summer vacations were usually spent at the New Jersey seashore where beaches were wide and white and each beach had well-tanned lifeguards strategically placed for safety. But, in 1935, when I was ten years old, my father decided we should vary our summer routine and try a vacation on Cape Cod. The beaches weren't the sort we were used to. Dad selected a public pier with a floating dock for our swim. We were practically the only people present and there were no lifeguards or boats in the immediate area that day. A float with a diving board was situated about twenty-five yards from the dock. I swam out to the float with no trouble, had a few dives, and then took a sunbath. When storm clouds began to gather, Dad signaled that I should return to shore.

I dove into the water and headed back. After swimming a half minute, I looked around. To my alarm, I was no closer to the dock. In fact, I was farther away! It dawned on me that I was caught in a strong tide that was carrying me out into Nantucket Sound. My family, standing on the dock, sensed my predicament. Dad looked worried but calm; my mother and sister were visibly upset.

Luckily, I was able to contain a rising panic. However, it was clear to me that drowning was a distinct possibility and I had better think of some way to save myself. One possibility would

be to just float with the tide, save my energy, and hope that someone in a boat would eventually pick me up. But there were no potential boats in sight. The other possibility was to swim faster and harder and try to make it to the dock. *I can do that*, I thought, and started to swim for my life. After a minute of intensified effort, I seemed to be a little closer to the dock. At this point, my family were shouting words of encouragement, but mainly they just watched my desperate struggle with the tide.

My adrenaline level must have been sky high, and I didn't become tired for several minutes. Fatigue finally did come fast and hard when I was about twenty feet from the dock. My arms and legs felt like dead weights and I was breathing hard. Should I rest a while and drift with the tide or try to muster more strength and keep going? I looked at the dock that was now so close, decided to keep swimming, and again thought, *I can do that*. Somehow, I found a supply of reserve energy, and in another minute or two, Dad pulled me out of the water.

It was a scary experience. In retrospect, I was grateful for my prior swimming instruction and

experience, thankful that I maintained my com-
posure, and satisfied that I seemed capable of
dealing with a major crisis. The I-can-do-that philosophy probably saved my life. If I hadn't persevered and been determined, I might not be here
today.

The I-can-do-that philosophy can come to *your* aid, too,
in many unexpected ways. The thing is to imbue it into
your subconscious so that, when in a crisis, such as the one
Phil found himself, you automatically go into a mode that
will pull you through. Just saying "I can do that" with
emphasis and vigor will give you the determination to accomplish whatever it is you want, hope, or need to do.

Take a break from your reading and choose one of the
projects on your list of want-to-do's. Think about it in-
tensely for a moment and then say: "I can do that!" Imagine that you absolutely must accomplish this project, that
your life depends upon it as did Phil's in his swimming
example. Say "I can do that!" again with all of the energy
you can muster. Think about the importance of this project
and the effect it will have on your life and future. Then
follow through on your I-can-do-that statement with perseverance and determination. Give it all you've got. You're
now more than halfway there. Intention of purpose and focusing on your desire is nine-tenths of the battle.

Marianna Nunes knew that perseverance and determination were the key elements in manifesting her lifelong
desire; she wasn't going to give up, regardless of how long
it took. Marianna had a goal; she sincerely wanted to connect with someone in a meaningful way. She not only
wanted a successful relationship, she wanted a happy, till-
the-end-of-time marriage. Being a busy, much-in-demand
speaker left her little time to connect with and meet appropriate men. There seemed to be only one way, the way
many professionals I know turn to when searching for a
new relationship, and that is the newspaper personals column.

So Marianna placed an ad in the local paper and, as she related to me, listened to literally hundreds and hundreds of voices of male answerers, using that method to qualify them by their voice or by what they said. "I actually met seventy-five to eighty men over a period of two years; no one was right for me. It was very discouraging," Marianna confided. "But I wasn't going to give up," she continued. "I knew the right guy was out there somewhere. It was just a matter of finding him, or of his finding me. And if it took listening to hundreds of voices, that's what I'd have to do."

In fact, she made so many calls to 900 numbers that the telephone company, thinking she must have children abusing the 900 number calling privilege, contacted her to see if she wanted to place a block on all 900 numbers. "No," she patiently explained. "I'm answering ads and listening to men's voices." Marianna was persistent. She persevered, knowing she was doing whatever it takes to find the right man.

> I answered one ad in 1994, but for some reason we never got together. Eight months later, I decided to write a letter to God telling Him what I wanted. Then, the man I didn't meet in '94 found my number again, and called me for a date. Coincidentally, one of my friends said, "Oh Marianna, you're so discouraged. Just give it up to the angels." When I got home from that date, one of my angels, the one on my kitchen windowsill, had fallen down into the sink. Obviously it was a heavenly sign. It was just amazing.
>
> We met in August and got engaged in September, but it was just this week that I showed him the letter to God, which I'd saved. In reading it over, I couldn't believe how accurate it was. He's everything I asked for, everything I ever wanted. I am so very happy.

And Marianna deserves to be; she is one of the warmest, most open and outgoing, friendly, and all-around beautiful individuals I've ever met.

Marianna summed up this experience by saying, "That incident gave me more confidence in approaching other areas of 'I can do' than anything else. I know that if I managed to manifest my career and my relationship, I can manifest anything I aspire to. I know now that whatever I want in life, I can manifest. It just has to be in the right time frame." Marianna did whatever it takes to launch her career and find her man, and I am thrilled for her.

Now let's put perseverance, determination, and doing whatever it takes to work for you so that you, as did Marianna, will manifest all of the things to which you aspire.

Your "I Can Do" Review

Review your list of hoped-for accomplishments. Ask yourself, "Have I done whatever it takes to achieve these goals?" List the goals in question here, and then answer the question in regard to each.

_____

_____

_____

_____

Now ask yourself what you can do that you haven't done before. List new "whatever it takes" ideas for each project, or at least those that are most important to you.

_____

_____

_____

_____

Ask yourself, "Have I really been perseverant and determined in pursuing these goals?

_____

_____

If not, why not?

_____

_____

Ponder This

Nothing can take the place of persistence. Talent will not; nothing is more common than unsuccessful men with talent. Genius will not; unrewarded genius is almost a proverb. Education will not; the world is full of educated derelicts. Persistence and determination are omnipotent. The slogan "press on" has solved and always will solve the problems of the human race.

—Calvin Coolidge

18

———— ∞ ————

What Are You Waiting For?

The Problem of Procrastination

Never put off till tomorrow what you can do day after tomorrow.

—Mark Twain

Procrastinate is kind of a devious word. "Pro" means "for" or "forward," both optimistic terms to me, and "crastinus" means tomorrow, which I interpret as "the future," also optimistic. But, when you put them together, they have the adverse effect of meaning "to put off intentionally and habitually, to postpone." Ah yes, how well I know! I think one of my biggest personal battles in life has been that of overcoming procrastination, particularly in decision making. That and paper clutter, which is a definite by-product of procrastination. If I would handle the paper, the bills, the junk mail, the correspondence, the clippings I collect, and notes to myself the first time they cross my desk, there'd be no clutter, no stacks of paper to overwhelm me. And, even more importantly, there'd be no repercussions to deal with resulting from postponed decisions or mislaid documents. Maybe even tax time would be a breeze, or at least easier, if paper procrastination became obsolete in my life. Well, I'm working on it; perhaps we can face it together.

Let's explore some of the reasons we all procrastinate.

"I don't feel like it" is one of my favorites, especially when it comes to things financial. Or, along the same lines, "I don't want to." It seems that at least half of the things we're compelled to do daily are things we don't want to do. Another similar excuse is "I'm not in the mood." Do you think you'll ever be? I know I won't. Chores, paperwork, paying bills, house and yard work, doing exercises, and obligations to others tend to bring on the "don't feel like it, don't want to, and not in the mood" excuses. Then tomorrow comes, as it inevitably does and, instead of being easier, the tasks seem to have grown in size and become more formidable.

What to do? Get ready for an overly simple answer. *Just do it!* Do it and get it over with. I'm a great list writer. I write all the things I have to do daily on a sheet of paper. Then, as I complete each unappealing item, I cross it off the list with a flourish. You have no idea what pleasure that simple act gives me!

Routine chores don't get put on the list, of course. Can you imagine writing down "do dishes" three times a day? Or, writing "clean the litter box," "walk the dog," and "do my exercises" daily? Many times I don't want to and don't feel like doing any of the above, but putting those chores off is out of the question, so I just do them. I certainly don't want to face today's dishes tomorrow or endure the guilts brought on by skipping other necessary daily activities, so I just do them. I'm big on giving myself rewards, however, such as a cool drink or little snack, after completing the items that seem particularly onerous.

These are just routine, daily chores about which we all tend to procrastinate. But what about your dreams, your goals, the things we've been talking about for seventeen chapters? Are you procrastinating about those vital and important areas of your life?

I've heard it said that a decision ignored or put off is a decision made, or something to that effect. And it's so true. That came home to me this week in a very costly manner. I'd been having trouble with my security system which, over the years, has turned out to be an expensive investment as I've added new coverage due to renovating and upgrading my house. Last week, the alarm started going off at unacceptable times—not that any time is acceptable for such a noisy neighborhood intrusion—but 3 and 4 A.M. is probably the worst. After thoroughly rousing the entire neighborhood twice in one night, I called in the technicians to correct the problem. A similar thing had occurred two months before, and the problem was supposedly corrected; at that time it was suggested that I take out a maintenance contract because systems tend to fail after time. The contract found its way into my stack of paper clutter and disappeared. After last week's 3 A.M. rousing, I retrieved the contract but was told that, since I hadn't signed it prior to the occurrence in question, the cost for the renovation of the system—and, on an hourly basis, who knows how much it might come to—was on me. Because the contract was not acted upon immediately but ignored, lost in the shuffle of paper, I will have to pay a substantial rate for the corrections to the system. A decision ignored was a decision made. An expensive lesson, indeed. I guarantee I will never, ever procrastinate again!

Maybe your procrastination in regard to your dreams and goals won't cost you dollar bills, but what will it cost you in other ways? Deep and profound disappointment in yourself? The knowledge that you've disappointed others close to you? Lack of self-respect for not following your heart? Inconsolable regret for things not done, dreams not accomplished? Will you go to the grave wondering ''what if'' or thinking ''if only?'' Please, don't let that happen to you. It's never too late to start.

Sidney's dream was to become a college professor. He spent the required years in college and grad school and had a good grade average, but when it came to writing his thesis, he couldn't seem to get around to doing it. Over twenty-five years have passed; he's married and has two children. ''Sid is so intelligent,'' his adoring wife told me. ''He absolutely should be in the classroom. He's wonderful with young people, and he has a remarkable way of making them thirsty for knowledge. One of these days, he's going to get to his thesis and realize his dream.'' Yes, one of these days. In the meantime, Sidney, now in his fifties, is indeed on the college staff; he's a custodian pushing a broom and mop instead of lecturing to the students.

It's still not too late for Sidney, because as long as we're living and have intense desire, it's never too late. But, if he's ever going to attack that thesis, wouldn't it be better for him to start today instead of putting it off until tomorrow, again?

Whether your dream is similar to Sidney's or totally different and uniquely your own, remember that the days march by relentlessly, no matter who you are or what your dream happens to be. If you want to realize it while you're still able to enjoy it, you must start now.

So, right now, this minute, stop and examine one of your dreams and goals. Then say to yourself, ''What step can I take *today* that will start me on the road to fulfilling that dream?'' We all know we can only take one step at a time and that it is the accumulation of many steps that brings results. So don't worry that your first step is only a baby step. Whatever size, it *is* a step toward your goal and that's what counts. Then give yourself a reward for taking that step; the first step is always the hardest, so you deserve to honor yourself for taking it.

When I was in high school and we all started dating, my friend down the block, Doris, began seeing Ed. After graduation, some of us married our high school sweethearts, and some married others. Doris and Ed continued dating, but marriage never entered the picture because Ed felt obliged to care for his widowed mother. Years passed, and Doris and Ed continued to be a twosome, with Mama the primary reason for their postponing marriage. When I went back East to my last high school reunion, I stopped in to see Doris; she still lives in the same house on my old street. I inquired about Ed.

''Oh, didn't I write you?'' Doris replied with a catch in her voice. ''Ed died last year. We had gone to the movies and came back here for a late snack. He sat down in front of the TV while I went into the kitchen to fix some sandwiches, and he simply expired of a massive heart attack. After forty years, I feel like a widow, too, even though we never married. I don't think I'll ever get over all those wasted years waiting for Mama to die.''

''And what about Mama?'' I asked. ''How is she getting along without her dutiful son, Ed?''

''Mama's doing very well, I understand,'' replied Doris ruefully. ''She plays bridge regularly a couple of times a week and goes to the movies with her lady friends. And, when she gets bored, she goes on trips and cruises. Evidently, Ed had a substantial insurance policy and left everything to Mama.

''We talked about getting married so many times,'' Doris continued. ''But Ed didn't think Mama was up to it; he worried about her heart. Isn't that ironic? So we postponed our wedding plans year after year. I guess you could call it procrastination—whatever. What difference does it make now?''

In this case it *is* too late for Doris and Ed. But it's not too late for Doris to get her life in gear and decide what she wants to do with it henceforth. Mama is having a great old time; Doris should, as well.

If you find yourself in a situation that seems hopeless, like Doris's does to her, brainstorm. Get out a sheet of paper and write down every single solution that comes to mind regarding your situation, regardless of how far out or outrageous it might seem. Let the list sit for a day, then read it over and decide to act on at least one of the ideas written down.

I did this exercise with Doris and one of the things I wrote down for her was to either answer an ad or place one in the local newspaper personals column.

''I could never do that,'' was Doris' shocked reaction.

''Why not? What have you got to lose?'' I questioned.

''Well, not much,'' she admitted. ''But it doesn't seem quite ladylike. I'll have to think about it.''

Another idea from our brainstorming session that seemed more ''ladylike'' to Doris was that she organize a group of mature adults with interests similar to hers for regular outings such as the theater, concerts, and gourmet dining. She was going to think about that as well.

Six months have gone by, and when I called Doris last week, she was still thinking about both options as well as some of the others we came up with. ''I guess I'm just a procrastinator, like Ed,'' she proclaimed. And then she added, ''But I'm so lonely. Maybe someone or something will turn up eventually to change things.'' For her sake, I hope so, but usually, if you want something to happen in your life, you have to be the instigator. You have to take the action to make it happen. Doris is waiting for someone or something outside of her to take the required action. She is not taking responsibility for her life.

If you want change in your life, you must take action

now. One action step is brainstorming. It's fun and enlightening and, surprisingly, it can offer unusual, workable solutions. The idea is to get your creative juices flowing. Don't evaluate, criticize, or ridicule. Just let the solutions spill out; write down every single crazy one. Let your list sit a day, as I advised Doris, then look at the list with a fresh eye. More than likely, there'll be several workable ideas there in front of you that you can institute immediately. This is one of my favorite methods when I'm faced with a sticky problem. One reason that I like it is that it allows you to live vicariously—to think of, and see yourself doing, outrageous things you might ordinarily discount. Then, ask yourself "Why not? Who said? Must I always act like Miss Proper?" Now is the time to stop procrastinating and take a risk; time to put some spice in your life!

Recently, I had the opportunity to hear a man who has to be one of the greatest motivational speakers on this planet, Willie Jolley from Washington, D.C. Before becoming a speaker, Willie was a well-known nightclub singer. I know that you've heard Willie sing because, in addition to performing in leading East Coast nightclubs, Willie's voice has been heard on literally dozens of radio and television jingles.

Willie Jolley is a man on a mission. He started speaking to children and young people—mostly troubled youngsters in inner-city schools—sometimes giving up to three speeches each day over a matter of years. His effect on these often belligerent kids is nothing less than miraculous. My personal feeling is that if Willie Jolley could be heard by all the young people in America, our problems with youth violence, drugs, and crime would immediately cease or at least diminish considerably. If you ever have the chance to hear Willie speak, do avail yourself of the opportunity. Willie says, "My motive is not to impress, but to inspire." Inspired you will be.

Willie calls himself The InspirTainer and he is that: inspiring and entertaining. The reason I'm telling you about Willie is because, like mine, his message is to follow your

dreams. Willie says that there are three "Dream Busters,"
as he calls them, that we all face in life. First, he tells us
that we are our own worst enemies when it comes to following our dreams. Our personal procrastination, which
we've been talking about in this chapter, can be a number-
one enemy. Secondly, Willie cautions us that hanging out
with negative, small-minded people can ruin our dreams.
"Do not listen to Dream Busters," Willie cautions and I
heartily concur. The third Dream Buster, according to Willie, is fear—being afraid to take a chance. "Fear is a
learned behavior," says Willie. "We come into this world
with only two built-in fears, those of falling and of loud
noises. All other fears are learned. You must control your
fears or they'll control you." Good advice. I especially en-

joyed his next question, "Why not go out on a limb—isn't that where the fruit is?" And that, my friends, is food for thought!

Could it be that Sidney was unknowingly afraid of achieving his dream and that's why he ignored his thesis? Definitely, Doris is afraid of taking risks in making new friends and relationships. Don't let fear come between you and your desires and dreams. Remember Willie's important warning: "If you don't control your fears, they will control you."

Perhaps procrastination is not your problem. You lead an organized life and make decisions quickly, thereby avoiding costly errors due to the "P" factor. Negativity is not an issue in your life or with those with whom you associate, and you approach risk with a healthy enthusiasm. I congratulate you! But there may be an area in which procrastination does play a part—a very important part, indeed—and I bring it up here for you to consider.

Do you procrastinate in sharing your innermost feelings with those dear to you? Do you regularly tell your spouse or significant other how much you love him or her? Have you ever told your parents the same thing, or how much you appreciate the sacrifices they've probably made, as well as all else they've done for you over the years? Are you loving and affectionate with your children as often as you're the strict disciplinarian that you must be?

"Oh, he/she/they must know I love them. I'm dependable, always there, not running around. I pay the bills/keep a tidy house/try to be a good companion/parent/(fill in the blank). What else do you want me to do?"

I want you to put it in words, not just on birthdays, anniversaries, Valentine's and Mother's and Father's Day when you allow Hallmark to do it for you. Flowers are great and "candy is dandy" as Ogden Nash said, but nothing can beat honest, sincere words. I want you to express your innermost thoughts and feelings in words *now* and often. If you can't bring yourself to voice the words, write a personal love note. One or both will undoubtedly produce all sorts of surprised and wondrous reactions. Procrastinate in other areas of your life if you must, but not this all-important one. When it is too late and you haven't done so, your regret will be so painful as to be unbearable.

Practice. Say "I love you," or "I care about you," or "You mean a great deal to me," or "I appreciate all you do for me." Say these phrases out loud. You may feel uncomfortable at first, even foolish. But believe me, your loved one will not feel uncomfortable or foolish; that individual will feel happy and appreciated and, most of all, loved. Do it for yourself, do it for the ones you love, and do it for me. Thank you.

Your "I Can Do" Review

If you tend to be a procrastinator, write down some of the ways in which you procrastinate.

_____

_____

_____

_____

Now note some of the things you intend to do to eliminate or cut down on your procrastination.

_____

_____

_____

_____

Take one of your dreams or goals and brainstorm ways of starting on the road to fulfillment today. Don't be conservative; let the ideas flow. Use extra paper if necessary.

_____

_____

_____

_____

Analyze Willie Jolley's three "Dream Busters." How many have you encountered while pursuing your dream? Have you encountered others?

_____

_____

Make a commitment now to express your true feelings to those you love. List those to whom you intend to say or send loving thoughts.

_____

_____

_____

_____

Ponder This

Procrastination is the fear of success. People procrastinate because they are afraid of the success they know will result if they move ahead now. Because success is heavy, carries a responsibility with it, it is much easier to procrastinate and live on the "someday I'll" philosophy.

—Denis Waitley

PART THREE

DOING IT

19

⎯⎯⎯⎯⎯ ∞ ⎯⎯⎯⎯⎯

The "Do It" Plan of Action

Decide and Implement

Since the mind is a specific biocomputer,
it needs specific instructions and directions.
The reason most people never reach their goals
is that they don't define them, learn about them,
or consider them as believable and achievable.
Winners can tell you where they are going,
what they plan to do along the way, and who will
be sharing the adventure with them.

—Denis Waitley

Now is the time for action. We've analyzed our dreams and goals and examined our excuses, fears, obstacles, and the pros and cons involved. We've discussed the need for caution, perseverance, and determination. We've acknowledged our accomplishments and admitted to occasional procrastination. We've come a long way together and gotten to know ourselves better. Now we're going to do something about all of this; we are going to act!

Most of the work is behind us. We've done our exercises along the way. Now we're going to pull the whole thing together.

To get started, I ask you to make a pact with yourself that you will do this, that you will carry it through. It's easy; all that is required is that you take the statement "I can do" and follow it thusly:

I—I will INITIATE and complete my "I Can Do" plan of action.

C—I COMMIT to COMMENCING and COMPLETING my plan of action with CONFIDENCE.
A—I will ACT and not procrastinate.
N—I will start NOW, today, to begin my plan of action.

D—I will DEFINE my goals and pursue them with DETERMINATION.
O—I am confident I will OVERCOME all OBSTACLES and reach my goal.

Signed_____Date:_____

I ask that you sign this contract with yourself and date it. I feel strongly about commitments, especially those you make with yourself. Once you sign this, you will be committed, you will follow through on your plan of action. It is a serious step; don't take it lightly. The choice is yours; I cannot make you sign this, thereby committing yourself to action. Only you can do that. You've come this far; you've had ample time to think about your desires, dreams, and goals. You've done the exercises along the way. This is decision time. Don't disappoint me. More importantly, don't disappoint yourself.

Okay, let's get down to business.

The "I Can Do" Plan of Action

1. Determine or define your dreams and goals in writing. As with affirmations, you must be very specific; vagueness brings vague results. List them in the order of importance to you. In defining your dreams and goals, ask yourself the following questions:

Have I clearly stated my goal or dream? Clarity is vital.

Is my dream or goal in the best interests of all concerned? Do not undertake any course of action that will adversely effect others.

Am I pursuing this dream or goal because I really want it, or merely to impress someone? You must want this with all your heart and soul.

2. Set specific time limits for these dreams and goals. These limits may have to be adjusted as time goes by, but it's vitally important to set a date to work toward or it becomes a matter of "one of these days," which is essentially procrastination. Again, if you set vague goals and vague time limits, you will get vague results.

3. Take dream or goal number 1 and determine what you can do today, not tomorrow, to start on the road toward achieving that goal. Baby steps are okay and to be encouraged. If you can take a giant step, that's even better, but *take a step today.*

4. Ask yourself who can help you along the way. Net-

work with those in the field or area you intend to enter. You'd be surprised how helpful people will be when they realize you are sincere in your desire. Ask a knowledgeable individual to be your mentor. Follow advice and model your efforts after the experts.

5. Make an irrevocable commitment to yourself that you will follow through, that you will do whatever it takes to attain your goal. Remember, an irrevocable commitment cannot be broken. Commit to not letting yourself down. This will reinforce your "I Can Do" Contract. If you have not yet signed your contract, do so now.

6. Pursue your goal relentlessly. Do not give up. This is your dream, your goal, and you are not going to let it slip through your fingers. You will, you must persevere.

7. Believe and have faith. Know that you will succeed.

8 Celebrate! Reward yourself each and every time you achieve a goal or make significant strides toward it. You deserve it!

9. Follow these steps for each and every goal on your list. Do them one at a time or simultaneously, whichever is more comfortable for you. Adjust or refine your goals along the way, if necessary, but do not give up!

10. Start now, today, this minute.

Ponder This

Until one is committed, there is hesitancy, the chance to draw back, always ineffectiveness. Concerning all acts of initiative (and creation) there is one elementary truth, the ignorance of which kills countless ideas and splendid plans: that the moment one definitely commits oneself, then Providence moves too. All sorts of things occur to help one that would never otherwise have occurred. A whole stream of events issues from the decision, raising in one's favor all manner of unforeseen incidents and meetings and material assistance, which no man could have dreamed would have come his way. I have learned a deep respect for one of Goethe's couplets:

Whatever you can do, or dream you can, begin it. Boldness has genius, power and magic in it.

—W. H. Murray,
The Scottish Himalayan Expedition

20

—∞—

Do It!

Final Words

*Destiny is not a matter of chance, it is a matter of choice;
it is not a thing to be waited for, it is a thing to be
achieved.*

—*William Jennings Bryan*

This is it. This is "D" Day—"Do It" Day! We've had
an interesting journey together. We've learned a lot about
ourselves along the way. We've touched on some sensitive
areas, explored new vistas and possibilities, and made major decisions about our lives and futures. Our dreams, desires, and goals have been defined. Some may have been
eliminated for one reason or another; others have emerged
or been born. We now know what we want and when we
can expect to reap the rewards of our decisions, dedication,
and efforts. I say "we" because we, you and I, have
worked together and we've made remarkable progress.

I hope you have enjoyed this exploration into your future; I know I have. Now you are on your own. Whether
you follow through on your personal "I can do" contract
and plan of action is up to you. I cannot do it for you,
much as I'd like to. The choice is yours. You are now at
the fork in the road. You can follow your "street of
dreams" toward success, achievement, and fulfillment, or
you can meander down the path of indecision and procrastination to wherever it might lead.

I will close with a quote that has been a powerful, motivating force in my life. When I first came across it, I felt that it must have been written especially for me. I scribbled it on a scrap of paper and stuck it on my bathroom mirror where it remains to this day. I credit it for nagging me at times and encouraging me at others. Every time I read the quote, which I do daily, it reminds me that "I can do that," whatever "that" might be—and, more importantly, that I had better do it now! I pass it along to you in the hope that it will also inspire you to do the things in life that are meaningful and important to you—and to do them now.

Ponder This

*Regret for the things we did can be tempered by time;
it is regret for the things we did not do that is inconsolable.*

—*Sydney J. Harris*

Please, do not let inconsolable regret for the things you did not do ruin your life. This is the first day of the rest of your life; this is the day that you can, you *must* begin to take steps toward the life and success you deserve *and can have* if you choose to *do it!*

Because we've made this very personal trip together, I shall continue to be concerned about your progress and would like to keep in touch. I invite you to write me about your successes, achievements, and the manifestation of

your desires through following the ''Do It'' Plan of Action.
Thank you. I look forward to hearing from you.
Sincerely,
Alice

Write to me at:
P.O. Box 10096, Oakland, CA 94610.